to Dr. Sandra
and advocate
look forward ... ... a book
you write in the future!

YOUR WHITE COAT IS WAITING

VITAL ADVICE FOR PRE-MEDS

[signature]

Kirsten E. Kirby, M.S.Ed.

William M. Kirby, M.D.

KIRBY CAREER ADVISING

Your White Coat Is Waiting

Copyright © 2019 by Kirsten E. Kirby & William M. Kirby

Published in the United States by Kirby Career Advising.

www.kirbycareeradvising.com

First Edition

ISBN-13: 978-0-578-49944-4

DEDICATION

To all of you who are working hard to become physicians – the ripple effects of the compassionate care you will provide to patients will touch the lives of so many people. You will truly make a difference in this world and we need you now more than ever.

CONTENTS

FOREWORD

I am happy to write this foreword to Ms. Kirsten Kirby's excellent book, *Your White Coat is Waiting: Vital Advice for Pre-Meds.* I have worked over twenty-five years in hospital and medical school administration, medical student advising, and being a medical school admissions committee member. I have interviewed hundreds of students and reviewed their records as they compete for the competitive world of gaining admission to medical school. While most have had sound advice from their pre-medical advisors, I have met a few who could have done things a bit differently.

I have known Ms. Kirby for many years and had the privilege of working with her when she was at the American College of Physicians in Philadelphia. She had served for several years as Director of Health Professions Advising at Franklin & Marshall College and actively participated in online forums such as "Advisor Corner" of the Association of American Medical Colleges. She also advised pre-med students at Johns Hopkins University, as Assistant Director of Pre-Professional Programs & Advising. I can therefore attest that she is supremely knowledgeable regarding the subjects of which she writes.

Ms. Kirby definitely hits all the right notes in describing what to focus on–and what not to focus on. Good credentials (GPA, MCAT, etc.) are important, but there are so many other factors involved in medical school admission: writing your personal statement, volunteer work, shadowing, and what you do with your leisure time are all important to the admissions committee. It's something that requires careful planning if you are to separate yourself from the pack come application time.

Also, becoming a physician is hard and a very long road. Just because someone has the intellectual ability to become a physician does not mean that he or she should. The most important question to ask yourself in this quest is: why do you want to become a physician? Can you articulate that to the admissions committee in a way that sounds authentic and not identical to the twenty other candidates present on your interview day? The last thing a school wants is to give a spot to someone who doesn't want to see it through in a year or too; they have quite an investment in their students.

If you are not suited for a career in medicine, you need to know that, too. There are many bumps and bruises along the winding road to become a doctor, and seeing someone drop out due to academic or other difficulties is something they (and you) want to avoid. Ms. Kirby describes in detail all the other qualities you need to have to be successful. Have you done meaningful shadowing, research, volunteering activities? Maybe you couldn't do as many of these things as your peers due to needing to hold down a job or having family responsibilities, but be prepared to discuss those things. Above all, she stresses that whatever you have accomplished, be honest about it and don't embellish–the committee members will see through that.

Doing a trivial amount of such activities in order to "check a box" demonstrating "yes, I did shadowing and research" isn't enough–it needs to be meaningful. This means starting early and not waiting until your junior or senior year to pack it all in, if that's possible (I know some applicants may not have decided on medicine until later in the undergraduate journey).

Many students want to get into medical school, and there are numerous other pre-med advising books on the market. To that end, what differentiates Ms. Kirby's book from the dozens of others available? I think one distinguishing characteristic is the author's eclectic background. Most such books I have encountered are written by scientists or health science educators/advisors whose primary background is the life sciences. That sounds logical, right? Who better to advise students on a medical career?

While there is nothing wrong with that, Ms. Kirby offers the perspective of a non-scientist with a scholarly background in liberal arts–particularly English and literature. You might ask why I would think that important–medicine is all about mathematics, physics, chemistry, and biology, correct? That's what most pre-med students are told, and these disciplines are indeed important to succeed in medicine, but there are so many other qualities necessary to become a successful physician. I would maintain that the task of medical school demands qualities far beyond the mastery of basic sciences, a fact that too often is forgotten.

Ms. Kirby's background also gives her a deep appreciation of the arts and humanities that I hope can be passed on to you. Most of us are taught little about writing skills, for example, other than our introductory courses as undergraduates. This relates not just to writing a good paper, but learning how to write really well. Communication skills are also essential–to your patient, likely more important than your grades in calculus or cell biology.

Another unique aspect of this book is the inclusion of practical "pearls of wisdom" by distinguished pathologist Dr. William Kirby (Ms. Kirby's father). The advice available from this experienced sage of medicine is not easily replicated. Their synergy yields a product that I am sure you will find engaging and effective.

I am sure Ms. Kirby's book will be useful to you and I hope you find it unique. I wish you the best of luck!

J. Matthew Neal, MD, MBA, CPE, FACP, FACE, FAAPL
Executive Medical Director, Academic Affairs
Chairman, Department of Medicine
Indiana University Health Ball Memorial Hospital
Muncie, Indiana

Assistant Dean for Faculty Affairs and Professional Development
Professor of Clinical Medicine
Indiana University School of Medicine
Indianapolis, Indiana

INTRODUCTION

Our goal in this book is to provide important tips that will help you build yourself into a strong candidate to apply to medical school and become a doctor. We focus on describing the different components needed for success including academics, experiences, and personal skills. As we share our advice, we also share real stories from our careers (Ms. Kirby as a pre-health advisor and Dr. Kirby as a pathologist) and identify pitfalls that can negatively impact your development as a candidate for medical school.

OUR STORIES

Kirsten Kirby

Since I was born while my parents were sophomores in college, I was present for every step of my dad's journey to becoming a doctor. We moved to different cities for each phase of his medical training, living in Hershey, PA for him to attend medical school at Penn State, New Haven, CT for him to complete his pathology residency training at Yale, and a year in St. Louis, MO so that he could complete a fellowship at Barnes Hospital. Throughout this time, our family continued to grow. My brother was born during my parents' senior year of college, one sister was born while my dad was in medical school, and my youngest sister was born while my dad was completing his residency. After spending 3 years in Springfield, IL, we moved to Delaware in 1996 for my dad to take a partner-track position. He has been with that private practice group ever since, achieving partner status in a pathology group that handles a huge volume of cases as part of the Christiana Health System. The moves were difficult at times, especially having to relocate half way through high school, but they also resulted in a lot of fun family adventures. I also saw the sacrifices my parents made to build my dad's career while making sure we had a good life as a family.

I never had any aspirations of becoming a doctor, having always been interested in creative fields including writing and music. Attending a liberal arts college felt like the best option for me since I would be able to explore my existing interests as well as discover others in a place that celebrates the life of the mind. I entered Smith College thinking I might major in music but ended up falling in love with Old English while taking a foundation course in literature. I majored in English with a concentration in Old English and Old Norse language and literature. Outside of the classroom, I held a number of leadership positions across campus. The most meaningful one was serving as a Student Academic Advisor (SAA) within my campus house of about 82 women and then as Head of the SAAs during my senior year. I began developing what has become the core of my advising philosophy, namely, reducing people's fear and anxiety about the path ahead of them by helping them become more knowledgeable and informed about their options.

After gaining acceptance to graduate programs at University of Pennsylvania and Harvard University, I chose to attend Penn where I earned a Master of Science in Education degree with a concentration in Higher Education Management. Through graduate assistantships in Career Services at Penn's Wharton School and at Swarthmore College (my parents' alma mater), I strengthened my advising skills and enjoyed helping people find a career that was the right fit for them. It was gratifying to help students create an action plan and ultimately achieve their goals.

A twist of fate during my first full-time job after graduate school pointed me towards health professions advising. I was serving as Assistant Director of Career Services at Franklin & Marshall College at the time and when their Director of Health Professions Advising left, many pre-health students came to our office seeking guidance. I ended up advising a number of them and found how much I enjoyed the work. This was also when my dad and I began having conversations about the health professions, specifically medicine, and what it takes to be successful. In 2008, I started to work at Johns Hopkins University as Assistant Director of Pre-Professional Programs and Advising where my sole focus was on pre-health advising. This work took on a deeper meaning because just prior to starting the job, I had a procedure to correct a genetic heart defect that had previously been undiagnosed. Being able to help the next generation of leaders in medicine moved from being a professional interest to a personal mission.

After my years at Hopkins, I went on to work with physician leaders at the American College of Physicians (the largest subspecialty professional association for doctors). Over time, I found that I missed advising undergraduate students and when a friend called to let me know he was moving on from his pre-health advising role at F&M, I applied for the position. I returned to F&M in August of 2014 and spent 3 years as Director of Health Professions Advising working with roughly 400 students and alumni in a range of health professions (75% of them were pre-med). It was very gratifying to hear that so many of my advisees were able to gain admission to medical, dental, vet, and other health professions schools. I am excited to share my knowledge with you in this book.

Dr. William Kirby

I come from a long line of doctors going back many generations. My father was a cardiothoracic surgeon and his identical twin brother was an infectious disease specialist. My father died when I was four so I never really knew him. Growing up we had a close family friend who was a surgeon and I gained insight into the demands and rewards of being a doctor through seeing how the career affected his daily life, holidays, and vacations. My discussions with him led me to consider medicine as a possible career.

Growing up I was very interested in biology and nature. In high school, I was most interested in biology classes. In addition to class work, I started working with one of the teachers helping him care for his animal collection that included mammals, fish, birds and snakes. Working with him I gained experience learning in depth knowledge of the different animals in the collection. This was my first experience of working with a mentor who increased my knowledge through our interactions and his example.

I went to Swarthmore College for my undergraduate education. I spent my first year taking social science classes. At the end of that year, I decided to pursue my interest in science and nature and become a pre-med. I struggled with some pre-med courses like physics and inorganic chemistry, and did well in organic chemistry and biology classes. I become aware of my strengths and weaknesses and tried to develop study methods to help in my weak areas. During this time I met my wife and we had two children (one of whom is the co-author of this book). This further made me develop study habits to maximize the effective use of my time. In addition to coursework, I did independent research with different professors. By working on projects in different fields, I got a broad exposure to the demands of doing cutting edge research. I did an independent immunology research project that I presented for a final grade. The research experiences furthered my appreciation for the value of working with mentors. It also made me interested in basic science and medical immunology.

As a pre-med I was able to watch a group of other students who were also interested in a career in medicine. I saw how a pre-med student's success depended on the decisions they made about what classes to take, who taught the classes they took, the course load they chose and their consistent study habits. My first advisor was a political scientist who was unable to give me any guidance as a pre-med. It took me a while to find a faculty member who could give me the constructive input that I needed. My experience at Swarthmore College also opened my eyes to the diversity of paths people took to reach medical school, including science and non-science majors, attendance at graduate school, or people who delayed applying while taking time off to do other activities such as Peace Corps or community service.

At the end of college, I stayed an extra year while my wife finished college. During this year, I took subjects such as biochemistry, did immunology research and worked as a teaching assistant. I considered applying to medical school but was discouraged by family, friends and professors who all said that medical school would be too demanding with a family. I chose to attend immunology graduate school at the University of Pennsylvania with the plan of attending medical school afterwards. I did well in classes and improved my record. After one and a half years, I decided to leave graduate school and do neuropathology research while I applied for medical school because I realized I really wanted to go directly into medicine. When I left graduate school, the same people who discouraged me from applying to medical school after college told me I was ruining my career. I decided to follow my instincts against other people's advice and was accepted into Penn State College of Medicine. During my first year in medical school, we had our third child. Contrary to all of the dire warnings I had received (from people who hadn't attended medical school!), the first two years of medical school were the easiest years of my adult life since I had already take almost all of the courses. The whole experience reinforced in my mind the value of persistence and following your own dreams.

I entered medical school already planning on a career in Pathology. This interest was solidified by working with a gifted faculty member who brought pathology to life by in depth case studies from his fellowship training at Memorial Sloan-Kettering Institute. I did my residency at Yale and Surgical pathology fellowship at Barnes Hospital in St. Louis. I was fortunate to work with two of the top pathologists in the world. They both had encyclopedic knowledge of pathology and other fields of medicine and taught me the critical value of pathology in patient care. They both emphasized learning general principles and extensive disease-specific knowledge so that I could diagnose cases from all fields of medicine.

Following residency, I have worked as a general surgical pathologist. The majority of my work involves microscopic analysis of specimens from the operating room and rendering diagnoses predominantly on cancer cases. I also perform autopsies, present the pathology portion of cases at multidisciplinary conferences and teach residents from several surgical subspecialties.

My path to become a doctor was a non-traditional one. I had a family in college, did a fifth year of college, went to graduate school and did research before going to medical school. I experienced being a pre-med both in college and graduate school and studied with many other traditional and non-traditional pre-meds. From these experiences I feel I have gained good insight into what makes a successful pre-med and what mistakes unsuccessful pre-meds make. I also learned the value of developing mentor relationships at all levels of training.

When my daughter became a pre-med advisor, we began comparing our experiences and discussed the process of pre-med education. We found many shared observations and also had different perspectives that expanded our understanding of the many paths to pre-med success and failure. This book summarizes our shared insights into what makes a successful pre-med student. We hope that these insights will benefit you as you navigate the challenging path you have chosen.

About This Book

We decided to write this book to help pre-med students avoid making mistakes and employ proven strategies to enhance their chance for success in getting into medical school. This book reflects more than a decade of conversations we have had about all aspects of medicine but especially the essential information pre-meds need to know. As our conversations continued, we realized that we both wanted to share advice with pre-meds in the hope that it would help them avoid major pitfalls and become the strongest applicants possible.

Since we are each sharing our insights, you will see sections and chapters called "Dr. Kirby's Diagnosis" which highlight his thoughts on a specific topic. The rest is written from Ms. Kirby's perspective as a pre-med advisor. This structure allows you to hear what we each think about different topics.

The information we present is useful for high school students who are considering medicine, collegiate pre-med students, and post-baccalaureate pre-med students throughout their pre-med careers, and parents seeking to learn more about the process. No matter where you are in your path to becoming a doctor, we hope that you finish this book feeling empowered, informed, and ready to turn your vision of putting on the white coat into reality.

PART I

PLANNING & STARTING THE

JOURNEY TO MEDICAL SCHOOL

· CHAPTER ONE ·

DECIDING WHETHER MEDICINE IS THE RIGHT CAREER FOR YOU

"I want to be a doctor." For some of you, this has been a lifelong dream whereas for others, you may have started thinking about this more recently. You may already be picturing yourself with a stethoscope and white coat on, ready to make a difference in your patients' lives. While this is a nice vision, you need to begin thinking about the long road ahead to reach this goal, starting with gaining admission to medical school. For many of you, this may feel especially intimidating if no one in your family has attended college and/or medical school. Even if you have parents who are physicians, they likely did their medical school training before many of the changes that have been implemented over the past decade.

Of any graduate or professional school admissions process, applying to medical school has changed in significant ways. It is not only more competitive to get in but schools are also looking for both breadth and depth in academics and experiences. Simply having both a high GPA and MCAT score is no longer a guarantee of admission. In conversations with medical school deans, many say that within their applicant pool, they routinely don't even interview over 400 students who have virtually perfect GPAs and scores. The national admissions data reflects this as well. According to a report published by the Association of American Medical Colleges, in 2017-2018 through 2018-2019, of the 4,743 applicants with above a 3.79 GPA and greater than a 517 on the new MCAT (97th percentile), 11.2% weren't accepted.[1] That means 530 students with very strong quantitative elements of their applications were not admitted. Why? Some may not have interviewed well whereas others may not have had the demonstrated commitment to entering the medical field.

The bottom line is that this is a career path you have to be firmly committed to and you need to take time to assess whether it is right for you.

Reflect on your motivation for wanting to become a doctor.

Simply put, why are you doing what you are doing? What is driving you to consider becoming a doctor? A critical part of examining your motives is assessing whether they are actually your own or whether they are coming from another source. For example, if your parents have always told you that you will be a doctor when you grow up, you essentially inherited this motive and may need to question whether it is still true for you today.

Is future lifestyle a motive? In terms of medicine, you need to really think about this. While in the long term, physician salaries are still strong, student loan debt, changes in practice models, and shifts in healthcare legislation at the national level are significantly impacting what doctors make. Also, depending on what specialty you choose, your earnings will be very different. Additionally, given the number of years of training it takes to become a doctor, you have to be okay with the fact that many of your friends are buying their first house, going on nice vacations, and spending money on other big ticket items while you are still a medical student or resident.

Recognize the difference between "Could I become a doctor vs. do I want to?"

J. is a brilliant student who I worked with beginning in her sophomore year. She had strong grades, completed a Neuroscience major and Italian minor, great research experience, numerous clinical experiences, and a lot of leadership and service activities. Throughout college, she had always been pre-med but beginning in her junior year, she began to question whether that was the path she actually wanted to pursue. Rather than forging ahead and applying that cycle in order to go straight from undergraduate to medical school, she decided to give herself time to answer the question of whether she still wanted to become a doctor. By the end of her senior year, she had decided that she wanted to pursue a doctoral degree instead of attending medical school and to devote her career to research. I was so proud that she had thoughtfully explored what was really right for her and I think she will make amazing contributions to research.

This former advisee is a perfect example of the question "Could I become a doctor vs. do I want to?" She absolutely has everything it takes to become a great doctor and I have no doubt she would have gained admission to several medical schools. Her decision to pursue a different career does not mean she "failed" or "gave up on her dream" but instead means she had the maturity and self-reflection to know that a different path was the right one for her. If you end up deciding medicine is right for you, great, but if you choose to pursue something different, that is also great. It is so much better to pick a career path that really fits you rather than doing something that doesn't align with who you are.

Assess your values, strengths, and areas for improvement (weaknesses).

It is vital to take some time and reflect on who you are and what career might be the best fit for you. When I have discussed this with students in the past, some of them feel this is a waste of time and that they have more important things to do. My response is that if I told you spending 10 minutes or less a day here or there would save you thousands of dollars and a lot of stress, would you do it? According to the Association of American Medical Colleges, 76% of students graduate with debt, the median debt for medical students in 2018 was $200,000, and 21% owe more than $300,000.[2] Given the financial ramifications, you owe it to yourself to spend the time to think about who you really are rather than blindly moving forward with a career idea that may or may not be yours to begin with.

How do you identify your core values? One excellent resource is the Values in Action (VIA) assessment through the University of Pennsylvania's Positive Psychology Center.[3] By completing a series of questions, the system will help identify your top 5 values.

Another way to think about your values is to ask friends, family, and others what a few words are that they would use to describe you. You can then compare these to how you would describe yourself. For identifying strengths and areas for improvement, you can write down previous times when you were successful or unsuccessful. Then, look at that list and see if you can locate patterns. Often if you can identify what you are good at and what causes you to struggle, you can make choices to increase your chances of being successful. So much of the journey to medical school depends on making good decisions so the more you know yourself, the better.

Learn about the difference options for medical training: allopathic medicine (the MD degree) or osteopathic medicine (the DO degree).

When people hear the word "doctor", they often think of a person who has been trained in and practices allopathic medicine. The National Cancer Institute's Dictionary of Cancer Terms defines allopathic medicine as "A system in which medical doctors and other healthcare professionals (such as nurses, pharmacists, and therapists) treat symptoms and diseases using drugs, radiation, or surgery. Also called biomedicine, conventional medicine, mainstream medicine, orthodox medicine, and Western medicine."[4] The degree earned by graduates of allopathic medical schools is the Doctor of Medicine (MD).

There is another pathway to becoming a doctor called osteopathic medicine. Dr. Andrew Taylor Still is considered the father of osteopathic medicine. It was the mid-1800s and he became concerned about the overall approach to patient care at that time (bloodletting, etc.). He was also motivated by personal loss. According to a biographical entry, "His first wife, Mary Vaughan, died in 1859 due to childbirth complications. In 1864 Still lost two of his own children and one adopted child to an epidemic of spinal meningitis; a month after the epidemic, the daughter born to his second wife, Mary Elvira Turner, died of pneumonia. His inability to save his family, coupled with his grim experiences as a Civil War doctor, led Still to reject most of what he had learned about medicine and search for new and better methods."[5] He started osteopathic medicine with what he considered to be a more holistic approach to caring for patients. This includes osteopathic manipulative treatment, which the American Osteopathic Association defines as: "a set of hands-on techniques used by osteopathic physicians (DOs) to diagnose, treat, and prevent illness or injury. Using OMT, a DO moves a patient's muscles and joints using techniques that include stretching, gentle pressure and resistance."[6]

According to the American Association of Colleges of Osteopathic Medicine (AACOM), there are currently 34 accredited osteopathic medical schools. On their website, they share: "In the 2016-17 academic year, colleges are educating more than 27,000 future physicians–more than 20 percent of U.S. medical students."[7] Graduates of these programs earn the degree of Doctor of Osteopathic Medicine (DO) and then go on to do residency training in their chosen specialty. AACOM also notes: "more than one-third of osteopathic medical school graduates choose careers in primary care."[8]

While there used to be a hierarchy in medicine with MDs at the top, DOs are now viewed in the same esteem at many academic medical centers and hospital systems. In major cities, DOs are often highlighted in commercials for different hospitals just as MDs are featured. Don't be surprised though if you still encounter MDs who have a more skeptical view of osteopathic medicine. Specific states and regions have a large number of osteopathic medical graduates while others, like the South, are just beginning to have more DOs as the result of several osteopathic medical schools opening in states including Georgia and Florida.

Additional evidence of DOs gaining prominence in the medical field is the transition happening with residency training. The American Osteopathic Association (AOA) describes the change that is currently underway: "The osteopathic medical profession is currently transitioning to a single accreditation system for graduate medical training. By 2020, all residency programs in the U.S. will be accredited by the Accreditation Council for Graduate Medical Education (ACGME). Both DO and MD students will be able to match into residency programs of their choice."[9] This is a substantial shift since historically, MD and DO residency programs were separate and were administered via two different systems. The AOA explains the advantages of this change: "It provides for consistent methods of evaluation and accountability, it enhances opportunities for all residents, and it enhances transparency to outside entities, including the federal government, licensing boards, credentials committees and the public."[10]

Osteopathic medicine should not be considered a "backup plan" if you do not gain acceptance to an MD program. It is important to understand that osteopathic medicine has different philosophical underpinnings and if you are interested in it, you need to spend time observing and speaking with DOs. Many osteopathic medical schools now require a recommendation letter from a DO so it is in your best interest to gain clinical experience with at least one osteopathic physician if you are even remotely considering this path in medicine. Doctors that DO, a campaign launched by the American Osteopathic Association, has a searchable database of DOs that you can use to locate physicians who you could then reach out to about shadowing opportunities.[11]

If you are considering offshore medical schools, do extensive research and speak to current physicians so that you understand the risks and potential limitations.

Sometimes when considering whether medicine is right for them, students think of the possibility of attending medical school in the Caribbean or another overseas location. While these pathways may seem appealing, they can come with a lot of risks and are often not the way to achieve your goal of becoming a doctor. We are not issuing a blanket statement that all offshore schools should be avoided; rather, we want to encourage you to do your research and know the facts. There are certainly some graduates of these medical schools who go on to be excellent physicians. The side you often don't hear about is that there are many students who do not complete their medical school training and then are saddled with loans they can't pay back or students who graduate from one of these medical schools and then do not match to a residency program. Additionally, some states do not recognize offshore medical schools if they are not accredited and then graduates of these schools cannot get licensed to practice medicine. Again, due diligence is the key and if after doing that research, offshore medical school is still an option you want to pursue, then you are making a decision based on calculated risks.

Read articles, books, and blogs written by physicians about their experiences.

There are so many remarkable physician writers who can give you valuable insight into what they have seen and learned. Dr. Atul Gawande is a surgeon who has written multiple books, is a staff writer for the New Yorker magazine, and has just been named as CEO of new healthcare company being developed by Jeff Bezos, Jamie Dimon, and Warren Buffett. His books include *Being Mortal: Medicine and What Matters in the End*, *The Checklist Manifesto: How to Get Things Right*, *Better: A Surgeon's Notes on Performance*, and *Complications: A Surgeon's Notes on an Imperfect Science*.[12] They all provide outstanding insight into different aspects of what it is like to be a physician. Dr. Danielle Ofri has written numerous books about being a physician, including *What Doctors Feel*, and her latest book, *What Patients Say, What Doctors Hear*.[13] There are also numerous blogs that feature content written by physicians and others in healthcare. One of my favorites is KevinMD.com, which, as their website notes, "shares the stories and insight of the many who intersect with our healthcare system, but are rarely heard from. Thousands of authors contribute to KevinMD.com: front-line primary care doctors, surgeons, specialist physicians, nurses, medical students, policy experts. And of course, patients, who need the medical profession to hear their voices."[14]

The bottom line is that these physicians' vivid writing about what they have gone through can help you begin to picture what medicine is like.

Road test the idea of becoming a doctor.

Like any good scientist, you should conduct experiments and gather data about whether medicine is the right career for you. The best way to do this is to immerse yourself in a medical environment by shadowing and/or volunteering at a hospital or clinic. Also, have conversations with physicians and ask them questions about how they chose this career, whether or not they would do so again, and why. Later in the book, there is much more information about ways to do this.

Choose your next step...

If at this point, you aren't sure whether medicine is right for you, you can read the chapter towards the end of the book, where we highlight a variety of other health-related careers. If you are set on becoming a physician, let's begin a closer examination of the skills you need to build and why they are important both as a pre-med and eventually in your medical career.

CHAPTER TWO

DR. KIRBY'S DIAGNOSIS –
TOP 5 SKILLS NEEDED TO BE A DOCTOR

A career in medicine can give you a very rewarding life on many levels. There is the satisfaction that comes from directly helping others heal their illness. There is the satisfaction that comes from working as part of a team with the shared common goal of helping people. There is the satisfaction of an academically challenging career that will always keep you learning. You can become involved in local or national groups to take part in the development of medicine in a world of new technology and ever-changing social conditions. You can live a financially stable life once your loans are paid for. You can enjoy the recognition associated with being a doctor and the sacrifices it represents. For all these reasons and more, the decision to become a doctor can start you on a path to a satisfying and rewarding life.

To enjoy the benefits of the life described above, you will have to make a commitment, which will affect all aspects of your life. It will affect your relationships, freedom and time and delay financial reward in different ways for the rest of your life. As a pre-med you will already have to make sacrifices that other students don't make, even though you are not guaranteed acceptance to medical school. You will have more class work with busy afternoons for the laboratory part of science courses. You will have to take a variety of courses that may not be in your areas of academic strength, which will require significant effort to achieve and maintain a GPA that makes you competitive for medical school. While other students can take a diverse course load, your choices will be limited by your requirements and the need to maintain a high GPA. You need to behave in a mature and responsible manner as your behavior and social media can be evaluated when you apply to medical school. During your summers, you will need to do research, shadow a physician, or do a similar project that demonstrates your interest in medicine and showcases your talent.

If you decide to become or are already a pre-med, your success will depend on your ability to achieve in academics, interpersonal communication, and extracurricular activities as well as having the mental and physical endurance to succeed. Many people are not suited for a career in medicine due to a failure to achieve in one or more of these areas. Some people have great academic ability but lack the discipline to maintain the commitment being a pre-med requires. Others may have great interpersonal skills but lack the academic ability. It is the ability to do well enough in the different areas that in combination will make you a successful pre-med and doctor.

To be a doctor, you must be proficient in many areas, including academics, public communication, personal interactions and mental and physical stamina.

Skill 1 - Academics/Learning

Your academic challenge begins in college where you take the required courses and electives you need to maintain a competitive GPA and perform well on the MCAT. This is the time when you learn your strengths and weaknesses and the method of study that is most effective for you.

In medical school you will be exposed to a large volume of material, covering many subjects with the challenge to be able to both read and retain the information and apply it to the treatment of patients. As a resident you continue to learn the information related to your field of choice. Once you become a practicing physician, you will have to continue learning as new technologies, new medications and new research findings will require you to constantly update your understanding and treatment of disease. You will need to recognize what is useful and relevant and then integrate it into your patient care.

The process of medical education is a sequential one. The first year is dedicated to knowing and recognizing what is normal in anatomy, physiology, genetics and all basic biological fields. The better one knows and recognizes normal structure and function in the body, the better-prepared one is to recognize variations from normal that manifests themselves as disease. In the second year, you learn the basics of disease and gain an understanding of different ways that normal can be changed through processes such as malignancy, infection and genetic diseases (malformation). In the third and fourth year you get a general exposure to different medical specialties and the types of diseases they treat and how they treat them. Based on this experience, you choose the field that is most appealing and then become proficient in practicing those skills as a resident.

When I look at a slide as a pathologist, I take a similar approach. At low magnification I look at the normal anatomy of the organ/tissue. I then look at the disease that is present and try to determine the mechanism of disease that is causing the abnormality. Once I have decided the likely mechanism present, I examine the tissue at higher power to see the cellular changes present. The different mechanisms will have characteristic features. For example, in infection, there can be acute, chronic or granulomatous inflammation and each will have a distinct appearance.

If I determine the process is a malignancy, I determine the type of tissue involved and the degree of abnormality. I can sometimes do this just looking at a slide while other times I use even more specialized analysis looking for characteristic protein expression with immunohistochemistry or molecular genetic analysis. At the end of the evaluation, I render a diagnosis that defines the disease present and the relevant information needed for treatment.

Skill 2 - Being Able To Speak & Communicate With Confidence

Communication is a central part of being a doctor. In your first two years of medical school, you will give presentations to small and large groups and be video-recorded interacting with patients. In your third year, when you do patient rounds on the floor you will be expected to give short bullet presentations to bring the treating doctor up to date with the most recent data on each patient. As a fourth year student and resident, you will have to be able to give clear, confident orders that other doctors and nurses can act on.

When you are a physician, you must be able to communicate with patients and explain their illness and treatment. You will need to direct your treatment team to carry out your instructions. You will have to be able to communicate with other physicians to discuss cases and develop treatment plans. Finally, you may present cases or research at local or national meetings.

Skill 3 - Being Comfortable Interacting With People From Diverse Backgrounds

Your ability to interact with different people will be crucial to your success. As a physician, you will work with a diverse group of people who make up the care team. In addition, you will be taking care of patients from very different ethnic and socioeconomic backgrounds.

Skill 4 - Physical and Mental Stamina

This skill is essential to be a physician. Starting in college, you work longer hours in class and do the studying and extracurricular activities needed to get into medical school. In medical school you will put in long hours in the first two years to learn the large volume of material. In the third and fourth years you go on the floors and begin taking night call in addition to the long daily shifts of the different services. During the nights and long shifts, you are expected to be able to perform mentally and physically at a high level at all times. This continues in residency as your responsibilities increase. Finally, as a physician you will have the demands of a busy daily practice, and night call, that lasts throughout the career of most physicians.

Skill 5 - Know Yourself & Hold Yourself Accountable

One very important aspect of your career starting as early on as high school is to begin to know yourself. This means you need to understand what your strengths and weaknesses are in all aspects of life. In academics you need to understand which subjects you are good at and which subjects are difficult. You need to figure out what strategies are most effective to learn difficult subjects. You need to figure out what time to study, type of study, and what study conditions work best for you. In the rest of your life you similarly need to evaluate your general strengths and weaknesses. What motivates you to perform well in all aspects of your life from work to your relationships with other people, to exercise and health? How disciplined are you in consistently performing tasks in your life like daily study, eating healthy food, getting good sleep and exercising? When you are having difficulty in some area in your life, what is your approach to making it better? Do you seek out help and advice and how good are you at making that advice work for you? How good are you at learning lessons from bad experiences and making the necessary changes to avoid those experiences in the future?

There are no easy answers to all of these questions and the answer will be different for each person. What is important is to begin evaluating your performance in the different aspects of your life. In usual day-to-day life, there are not many changes so at the end of each week you can reflect on the week and how you performed. You can start a weekly journal to document your successes and failures so that you can start to learn what makes you successful and how to maintain it. In addition to the day-to-day challenges of life, there will also be unique events such as giving a lecture, difficult relationships, injury or illness. When approaching unique circumstances, evaluate how you prepare for them and how you act during the event. Following the event, try to evaluate what your strengths and weaknesses were so you are better prepared to handle future unusual experiences. After they occur, try to figure out what you did well and what you could do better in the future. The better you are able to know yourself and what works for you in daily life and during times of adversity, the more successful you will be if you become a doctor.

The process of becoming a doctor gives you the daily challenge of performing at a high level and many unique experiences. Starting in your third year of medical school you will be performing physical exams and doing procedures on patients. A typical teaching technique on the floors is "See one, do one, teach one". You will be expected to perform a new procedure such as putting in an IV after being shown how to do it once or twice. You will have to examine patients daily, give presentations to the medical team, and participate in the care of patients. This work will have routine daily features but will also have critical events like when patients have a cardiac arrest or stroke. To succeed as a doctor, you must be able to maintain a daily level of quality work and perform well in pressure situations. The better you have learned how to know yourself by evaluating your strengths and weaknesses in college, the more successful you will be at meeting the challenges of being a doctor.

When I perform autopsies, it is a similar process. The information on the patient's past medical history and treatment is evaluated to gain an understanding of the patient's history. Then when I perform the autopsy I see the physical changes from the many different diseases. Usually many organ systems will have chronic changes reflecting daily diseases such as diabetes, chronic vascular disease, or lung disease from smoking. In addition, there can be acute events like a heart attack, stroke, or pulmonary embolism that are an identifiable acute cause of death. I provide a report that documents acute and chronic diseases that are present as pathology within the patient. This information then goes to the physician so he or she can evaluate the success of treatments and, if possible, understand the cause of death. This is a similar process to what I have outlined above where you evaluate the cumulative results of daily and acute events to gain a better understanding of your own problems and insight into what to do differently, or better, in the future.

Another important aspect of knowing yourself is to become a strong advocate for yourself. The better you know yourself and what works for you, the more aggressively you can seek out situations that fit your abilities and personality. Your college career will have many challenges like not getting a good advisor or professors who want students attend graduate school rather than medical school. You have to be ready to meet these challenges and put yourself in the best position for success. Don't accept bad situations. Aggressively try to achieve a better situation like changing advisors or dropping classes. If you have a roommate that you don't get along with, don't just accept it; try to switch to a better situation. You must try to create the best environment in which to succeed based on what works for you.

If you have decided to make the commitment to becoming a doctor, there are a number of things you can do in college that will make you a more effective pre-med and then a successful medical student and doctor. In academics (this is covered more later), as you take different courses, you can focus on skills you need for the future. The first skill is to figure out what is the most effective way of studying for you. Everyone is different and learns in different ways. In your first year you should try different strategies to see what works for you. During this process you should figure out what study methods enable you to learn and retain large amounts of information. You should also learn how to understand basic concepts and how the information you learn fits into them. By the end of the first year, you will hopefully have mastered your study techniques so that from that point on, your efforts can go solely into learning. As you take more courses, especially in your major, see how fundamental concepts in different courses overlap. If you can leave college knowing how to study, learn, and retain information and understand and apply fundamental principles, you will be well prepared to excel in medical school.

For personal communication, like learning, the key is finding out what makes you most comfortable when communicating with other people. Some people, when making presentations, like making a script. Others prefer reading off of a PowerPoint presentation. Some even use medications like beta-blockers to relieve the symptoms of being nervous (do not take any medication without consulting your physician). You must communicate with confidence so the sooner you develop this ability, the better. Take advantage of opportunities to do public speaking in class and other areas where you can participate in public forums. The ability to comfortably do public communications will make medical school and medicine much easier for you.

Regarding endurance, it would be useful in college to choose a form of exercise and meditation or mental focus that you really enjoy and are comfortable with. Regular practice in these areas will build the physical and mental stamina needed to be a physician. By choosing practices that you enjoy, you can make it part of your daily discipline. These practices will also be a healthy way to reduce stress throughout your studies and career in medicine.

For each of you, your path to medical school will be very different. Some will follow the traditional path from college to medical school, while others will do postgraduate studies or enter a post baccalaureate pre-med program. Whatever your path is, it will be your persistent daily commitment to developing your skills that will make you a competitive medical school applicant.

Now that you have decided you want to become a doctor and know the core skills needed, it's time to learn about how to build them during each phase of your education.

CHAPTER THREE

WHAT TO DO IN HIGH SCHOOL

Build a strong academic foundation in science, foreign language, and humanities.

This step is critical in terms of your ability to get into a good college and then succeed while there so that you have a GPA that helps you be competitive at more medical schools. It is also a good time for you to work on strengthening areas you may not be very good at yet or don't like. If you say you don't like a particular science subject but if you are serious about going to medical school in the future, you need to at least learn to tolerate that subject enough to do well in it.

Why Math matters

Math is a subject many doctors will say doesn't really matter in the long run but the reality is that general chemistry has elements related to math. Physics does as well and most colleges teach calculus-based physics and/or algebra-based physics. It is a good idea to take several math classes during high school, including Pre-Calculus or Calculus 1. Don't skip this during your final year of high school because it is likely that you will be taking general chemistry and/or a math class your first year of college.

Gain exposure to the major areas of science

Since most medical schools require biology, chemistry, physics, and in some cases math, high school is a good time for you to experience these subjects first-hand. If you thrive, that's great but if you don't, this is an opportunity to diagnose any underlying causes of why you are not performing well. Is it lack of interest? Not taking enough time to read questions on exams? This is also a good chance for you to see whether or not you actually like science classes. If the answer is no, that's ok but it may mean shifting your career focus to other fields. There are wonderful opportunities to do great work related to health but with less of a focus in the natural sciences.

Work on your writing and language skills

As a future pre-med, it is tempting to take a lot of science courses and not study subjects such as English and foreign languages. Don't make this mistake! Starting to develop your writing skills early on will enable you to prepare for college coursework. Since medical schools require a year of college-level English, this is a good skill to work on early and often. In terms of foreign languages, many colleges have a language requirement you have to fulfill in order to graduate. Getting a head start on this in high school and then taking introductory language courses in college is a way to fulfill the requirement and earn high grades.

Start working on your standardized test taking skills.

Doing well on these types of tests is now an essential skill you will need throughout your career in medicine. Many of you have to take your state standardized tests every year and you can use these as a way to develop your test taking skills. Also, you should plan on taking either the SAT or ACT, even though these are now optional to apply for many colleges and universities. First, preparing for these exams gets you into the mindset you will eventually need for tests like the MCAT. Second, some medical schools that have early assurance programs where you can apply during your sophomore year in college require SAT or ACT scores.

Begin gaining clinical, volunteer, and other experiences.

Many future pre-meds think they need to load up on shadowing and/or hospital volunteer work as high school students. While this is helpful from the standpoint of seeing whether you like medicine and whether becoming a physician is the right fit for you, these hours won't count towards your application to medical school in the future. They want to see what you did in college, not high school.

Volunteer work that is non-medically related can be very helpful. It is a great way to learn how to relate to and communicate with people from all walks of life. Many of you are required to do some kind of service in order to graduate from high school. Look at this as an opportunity rather than something you dread.

Pursuing areas of interest and hobbies is also a good idea. Playing a sport is a great way to cultivate teamwork skills, time management, resilience, and other qualities. If you are a musician, the discipline it takes to practice consistently and the ability to learn new music are helpful skills. Both undergraduate institutions and medical schools often look for exceptional qualities outside of academics so pursuing these interests can be very valuable to you.

Develop good relationships with teachers and others, which will lead to strong letters of recommendation.

As part of both the college and medical school application process, you will need letters of recommendation from teachers/professors, volunteer supervisors, and others. During high school, it is a good idea to start cultivating relationships with your teachers and getting over any fears of speaking with them. Your recommendation writers serve as important voices during the application process so you want to make sure they know you well enough to write more than just "the student got a good grade in my class."

While you won't be able to use any high school letters of recommendation for medical school, you are practicing the skill of interacting with faculty. Many college students don't speak with their professors unless they are struggling in a class. The reality is that building relationships with professors will greatly enrich your undergraduate experience. We'll discuss this more in a later section of the book.

Understand the difference between a liberal arts college and a research university.

The main types of institutions pre-medical students consider are liberal arts colleges and research universities. It is important to know the similarities and differences between the two. Both will enable you to complete the prerequisite classes for medical school but you will find that they differ in several key areas.

Academics

Liberal arts colleges do not have extensive graduate degree options and as a result, professors teach classes. Your classes will tend to be smaller, which means you get more opportunities to interact with professors but also means you have to come to class prepared and can't blend into a huge class. Your exams will primarily be short answer rather than multiple choice, which can mean that you need to practice the MCAT format more since you are not comfortable with the format. At research universities, your introductory science courses will likely be on the large side in the lectures. Graduate students rather than faculty members may teach labs. Given the size of the class, your tests will probably be multiple choice since those can be graded via computer. Having taken this format of test over a several year period, the MCAT format will be more familiar to you.

At liberal arts colleges, you will study diverse subjects and gain both breadth and depth. There are usually no pre-professional majors such as Anatomy & Physiology or Exercise Science. Instead, you can major in any subject and still complete the prerequisites for medical school. Declaring a major typically happens during your sophomore year. Research universities often have you specialize earlier in your college career and sometimes even require you to apply to your major. You may have fewer general education classes depending on the school and spend more time taking classes in your major.

Research Opportunities

In labs at liberal arts colleges, only undergraduate students will be there and get to work directly with a professor rather than with a graduate student. This may enable you to get more research experience than you would at a university. Research universities may have postdoctoral students, graduate students, and undergraduate students in their lab. Bigger, high power labs may have more grant funding and newer, more high tech equipment.

Clinical Opportunities

If a research university is part of a system that also has an academic medical center (medical school, hospital, etc.), then students might have more clinical options that have already been created. Liberal arts colleges often partner with local hospitals to offer shadowing and volunteer opportunities.

Consider whether BA/MD and BS/MD programs would be the right fit for you.

Through relationships between undergraduate institutions and medical schools, these programs offer a provisional medical school acceptance as you matriculate to college. You earn your Bachelor of Arts or Bachelor of Science degree and then after graduating, you go directly to the medical school that has partnered with your college/university. The application process is much more in-depth than just applying to college and if you are accepted, you must achieve certain criteria set forward by the program in order to move on to that specific medical school after college. For example, some programs require maintaining a certain GPA and/or meeting a certain threshold score on the MCAT. The danger here is that if you fail to meet the criteria as you go through college, the medical school may rescind your acceptance.

While these programs can be a good fit for some students, they are not right for everyone. If you want the flexibility to apply to multiple medical schools, then this type of program is not the way to go since it locks you into one school. Also, if you are on the fence about whether medical school is right for you, it is better to attend a college/university where you can solely focus on your undergraduate degree without having the pressure of meeting the benchmarks set forth to retain your provisional acceptance to medical school. The Association of American Medical Colleges has more information about this topic, including a list of programs[1] and some profiles of students who chose to pursue them.[2] Do your homework and decide whether applying to these programs is something you want to pursue.

Choose a college that is a good fit for you and where you can succeed in and out of the classroom.

As a pre-med, you have a lot of choices in terms of where to go to college. You need to reflect on your strengths and weaknesses as well as factors like what environment would be best for you (city vs. suburbs vs. rural, size of school, etc.). Asking for a college or university's acceptance rate to medical school is actually not that helpful. Most schools will present their admissions data in the best light possible and will typically say their admissions rate is in the upper 80s to low 90s in terms of percent. Generally this is based on a set of criteria the school defines (for example, a certain science GPA, cumulative GPA, and MCAT score). The website of the pre-professional or pre-health office and/or the admissions office usually lists this percentage.

Here are several much more important questions to ask:

- What is the total number of pre-med students at this school? How many students start out as pre-med and then how many end up applying?

- What is the ratio of pre-health advisors to pre-med students?

- How is academic advising structured for pre-meds? Specifically, how do I get the right guidance on what to take, especially during my first two years?

- How often do pre-meds at this school get the schedule they need both to complete the prerequisite coursework for medical school and their major?

- Are there any restrictions on what classes students from different majors can register for? As an example, if I am pre-med but a Spanish major and I want to take Biochemistry, will I be shut out if I am not a Biology major?

- What kinds of research experiences do students at this school have access to?

- Does the school have opportunities for students to gain clinical experiences?

- Is MCAT prep offered and if so, what does it consist of?

- Does this college or university have a Committee process where I can receive a letter written by the institution on my behalf? If so, are there certain criteria for who does/doesn't get a letter, or do all applicants receive one?

As an elite student, you will likely have multiple acceptances to college so you need to think long and hard about where you can achieve at the highest levels and do your best work.

Dr. Kirby's Diagnosis - What to Do in High School

High school is a time to get exposed to many different things through classes, extracurricular activities, and summer vacations. This is a great time to experiment with many different experiences to figure out what you like both academically and in your life. If possible, it is useful to get experiences in large cities as well as in smaller towns. You should seek out experiences that are challenging and make you more confident and outgoing. Most people in high school don't know what they want to do and the more experiences they have, the better they will be able to make a good decision about where to go to college.

Some students already know in high school that they want to become doctors. Many more are uncertain but are considering medicine as a possibility when they enter college. If you think you may want to become a doctor, then it is critical that you choose a college or university that is best suited for your personality and ability.

There are several key factors to consider when choosing a college. The first is location. You need to choose a location you are comfortable with. If you are from a small town, then going to college in a large metropolitan city may be overwhelming. The prospect of living in a big city may seem exciting but you will be confronted with many new things to get used to. Remember, you are going to college to learn academics and excel: you are not going to college so that you can learn how to live in a big city. You must be comfortable with the environment you live in. If you are unsure, lean towards a small city or town. You will likely live in a city during medical school or residency: your goal is to get there.

Another critical decision is the size of the school and whether it is a college or university. Colleges tend to be smaller with few graduate students. The advantage of this is that you will have smaller class sizes with more direct interaction with faculty. In a smaller school, there will be less pre-med students and the schools will typically not use introductory classes to weed out pre-meds. Since the smaller schools have less pre-meds, the schools are better able to be advocates for their applying students. Since you work closely with faculty, you can get good recommendations from professors who know you well.

Large schools typically have many pre-med students in the freshman class and use introductory courses to weed out students who struggle. The result is they have a smaller group of upperclassmen in science majors and applying to medical school. For many of these introductory classes, the laboratory sessions and some of the classroom teaching will be done by graduate assistants whose time is split between their own coursework/research and teaching. You will often have very limited interactions with faculty. Since the goal of these classes is to weed out pre-med students, they are often strictly graded with limited curves. It takes time for many students to adjust to college. Since the goal of the introductory classes is to weed out pre-med students, some will find their pre-med career is over by the end of their first semester. Universities can offer good research opportunities for upper-level students in their majors but these can be limited by the number of graduate students in those labs. If possible, it is important to learn what upper level students are doing in their majors.

Try to be realistic about your academic abilities. You may be the top student in your high school class, which makes you eligible to enter some of the top colleges/universities in the country but you may be overwhelmed by your peers' abilities if you attend an elite school. Using the schools' admissions websites and other resources, look at the high school GPAs, SATs, and extracurricular activities of the most recent incoming class and how you compare. Remember your goal is to show medical schools that you are capable of achieving at a high level and becoming a doctor. If you are able to excel at a top college or university, that is great. If you are not sure, you may be better off going to a school where you know that given your abilities, you will be a top student.

If you want to be pre-med, you need to know how successful pre-meds are at that school. Do the basic science faculty have a positive or negative attitude towards pre-med students? This can greatly affect how you do in introductory and upper level classes. What percentage of students that enter the school as pre-meds are pre-meds in their senior year? What percentage of pre-meds who apply to medical school are actively supported in their application by their school? Is there a pre-med society or club at the school and how active is it? In the basic sciences, what research opportunities are available for students? Are alumni doctors available for shadowing during summer vacations? Is there a dedicated pre-med advisor who can help advise you from the first day of your freshman year so you avoid mistakes from the beginning? The more informed you are about the schools you are applying to, the better choice you will make.

If you do your research and choose the school that best suits you for location, size, academic demands and positive pre-med environment, you will greatly increase your chances to succeed. Overall, I think students are better off at a college rather than a university during their undergraduate years. The direct teaching by faculty, smaller class size, and opportunities to work with faculty make for an ideal learning environment. The key is to choose a place where you feel comfortable and can excel or you may greatly decrease your chances of becoming a doctor before you even start your freshman year.

CHAPTER FOUR

PRE-MED PATHWAY *&* TIMELINES
FOR COLLEGE STUDENTS

At over a year long, the application season for medical school is one of the longest of all graduate programs. If your goal is to go straight to medical school after finishing your undergraduate years, you will be applying to medical school during the summer after your junior year of college. A popular choice now is to apply to medical school after graduating and have a year of opportunity (some call it a gap year) during which you are applying. If you decide later on in college that you want to go to medical school, a third option is applying later after completing a post-baccalaureate program (this topic is covered in more depth in Chapter 5).

So many pre-meds and their parents are under the impression that there is only one timeline in order to go to medical school. They think that virtually everyone who goes to medical school does so right after college. The reality is that depending on the medical school, now between 60-70% of their incoming class has been out of college for at least a year before matriculating to medical school. In a 2015 article in the Harvard Crimson, Robert J. Mayer, faculty associate dean of admissions at Harvard Medical School, describes the significant shift in when people go to medical school: "When I was a student, 80 to 85 percent of people at Harvard Medical School came directly out of college," Mayer said. "I've been in the role of leading admissions for about 11 years. [When I first started], about 60 percent were coming out of college. Now, it's about 35 percent."[1] The national data from the Association of American Medical Colleges also demonstrates this, noting that the mean age of applicants at anticipated matriculation has been 24-25 every year since 2013-2014.[2]

Not only is the idea that everyone goes straight from their undergraduate years to medical school incorrect, it can be dangerous. For example, if you push on in a course when you are clearly in over your head but you keep going because you believe, or someone tells you, that you will be behind, you could do significant damage to your academic record. Some applicants try to take the MCAT before they have even finished some of the coursework with content on the exam and then get low scores as a result. If you choose to apply before you have the necessary academic background and experience, you will be spending a lot of time and money and then not gaining admission. You don't get points for speed; in fact, when medical schools see evidence of poor decision-making, it can be a cause for concern.

Application timeline if you plan to matriculate to medical school right after graduating from college

For those of you wanting to go straight to medical school, you would begin the application process in the spring of your junior year, take the MCAT and submit your AMCAS application early during the summer between your junior and senior year, interview throughout the fall and early spring of senior year, decide on which one acceptance to keep by April 30th of your senior year, graduate in May, and then start medical school that July or August.

For the following sample timeline, this applicant will be graduating in May 2021 and plans to matriculate to medical school in August 2021:

Fall 2019	Start junior year of college
Fall 2019/Spring 2020	Complete Committee process if your school offers a Committee letter; request letters of recommendation
May 2020	American Medical College Application Service (AMCAS) opens; create your account and begin working on it
June 2020	First chance to submit AMCAS; they will then double-check courses against what you entered and will calculate your GPA. You should also plan to take the MCAT no later than the end of June.
June - August 2020	Complete and submit secondary applications
Fall 2020	Start senior year of college
Fall 2020 to End of March 2021	Interview season
April 30th, 2021	Deadline to decide which one acceptance you want to keep
May 2021	Graduate from college
July/August 2021	Start medical school

Application timeline if you plan to matriculate to medical school a year after graduating from college

Those of you who apply after senior year have more options in terms of MCAT timing. For example, if you have completed all of the prerequisite courses by the end of your junior year, then you could spend the summer before your senior year studying for the MCAT while also gaining clinical experience, completing research, or another activity. You could then take it in late August/early September. Another option would be January of your senior year. You would want to take the MCAT no later than June right after you graduate.

For the following sample timeline, this applicant will be graduating in May 2020 and plans to take a gap year and matriculate to medical school in August 2021:

Fall 2019	Start senior year of college
Fall 2019/Spring 2020	Complete Committee process if your school offers a Committee letter; request letters of recommendation
May 2020	Graduate from college; begin gap year (see tips below on options)
May 2020	American Medical College Application Service (AMCAS) opens; create your account and begin working on it
June 2020	First chance to submit AMCAS; they will then double-check courses against what you entered and will calculate your GPA. You should also plan to take the MCAT no later than the end of June.

June – August 2020	Complete and submit secondary applications
Fall 2020 to End of March 2021	Interview season
April 30th, 2021	Deadline to decide which one acceptance you want to keep
July/August 2021	Start medical school

Application timeline if you plan to matriculate to medical school two years after graduating from college:

I have started to see an uptick in the number of students choosing to take two years between college and matriculating to medical school. The advantage of this option is that you get a full year after college before you apply to gain experience that can strengthen your application and you have more time to study for and take the MCAT. Your second year, you are still working or engaging in different opportunities while applying and interviewing.

For the following sample timeline, this applicant will be graduating in May 2020 and plans to take two gap years and matriculate to medical school in August 2022:

Fall 2019	Start senior year of college
May 2020	Graduate from college; begin first gap year (see tips below on options)
You could take the MCAT any time from June 2019 to June 2021.	
Fall 2020/Spring 2021	Complete Committee process if your school offers a Committee letter; request letters of recommendation

May 2021	Begin second gap year
May 2021	American Medical College Application Service (AMCAS) opens; create your account and begin working on it
June 2021	First chance to submit AMCAS; they will then double-check courses against what you entered and will calculate your GPA. You should also plan to take the MCAT no later than the end of June.
June - August 2021	Complete and submit secondary applications
Fall 2021 to End of March 2022	Interview season
April 30th, 2022	Deadline to decide which one acceptance you want to keep
July/August 2022	Start medical school

For those of you who plan to take time between college and applying and matriculating to medical school, consider your options for these year(s) and make the most of that time.

There are a number of very productive ways to spend the time between graduating from college and matriculating to medical school. I have never liked the phrase "gap year" because it implies that there is a giant hole between one phase of your education and the next. I like "year of opportunity" or "bridge year" or basically any term that doesn't sound like you're in pre-medical purgatory!

Here are several broad categories and specific examples of how you can spend that time:

Fellowships

If you have always wanted to spend time abroad and/or working on a dedicated project, you can consider applying for fellowships such as the Fulbright. You spend a fully funded year abroad working on a research project or teaching. I have had advisees complete research fellowships in countries such as Costa Rica and others served as Teaching Fellows in countries including Poland. In terms of interviews, you can schedule time to come back to the U.S. and then go back abroad. Get in touch with the Fellowships Coordinator at your college/university to discuss whether applying for fellowships might be a good option for you. If you are interested in this option, you need to plan ahead since many of the application deadlines are in early fall.

Graduate degree programs

Some students choose to complete a Master's program, often to strengthen their science credentials for medical school. I have also had students who wanted to pursue graduate degrees in the arts or humanities, knowing they would not get the chance to do so during medical school. My advice is to reflect on whether you really need/want to complete a graduate degree at this point, given that you will likely have to take out loans to do it.

Research Jobs

Many of my advisees have spent time working in basic science or clinical research positions. If you enjoy lab-based research, then opportunities such as the Intramural Research Training Award program at the National Institutes of Health might be worth applying for or you can look at positions at academic medical centers. For example, one of my former students worked in a full-time position at the NIH completing cancer research using mice. Especially for those of you considering an MD/PhD, gaining additional research experience can help you become a more competitive applicant

For those of you who are more interested in engaging in clinical research, there are numerous positions available at academic medical centers and often in hospital systems as well. To find these positions, go to the Human Resources website of different academic medical centers (for example, Penn) and then search for positions such as Clinical Research Coordinator. Every place calls these positions something slightly different so another option is just to look at all jobs within the medical school or hospital. Former advisees have worked on epilepsy clinical trials, kidney patient research, and many other projects. These positions often have a high level of patient interaction as well as the chance to work closely with the physicians and scientists running the clinical research projects.

Clinical Jobs

Clinical research (which I referred to above) can have a strong patient-facing component but there are a number of other jobs you can consider as well. One is serving as a medical scribe, where you are essentially a physician's right hand person in the exam room. You capture all of the notes and comments the physician makes and add it into the electronic health records. Depending on the clinical setting, some scribes get to assist with taking a patient history and performing basic checks such as blood pressure. One caution with this job is that sometimes scribes are overworked and underpaid or may not get as much of a chance to spend time with patients. If you find yourself in more of an administrative role rather than being with the doctor when s/he is working with patients, then you may want to make a change.

National Health Corps is an excellent option if you want to spend a year directly working with patients. This program, which is part of AmeriCorps, currently operates in Pittsburgh, Philadelphia, Chicago, and North Florida. Their mission is to foster "healthy communities by delivering and connecting those who need it most with health and wellness education, benefits and services, while developing tomorrow's compassionate health leaders."[3] One of my advisees spent a year in Philadelphia working in clinics that treated underserved patients, including undocumented immigrants. He then served in the Chicago Corps, where he performed eye exams and treated children for a variety of vision conditions.

Another clinical option is working at an elderly care facility. Some of these settings will provide you with training needed to interact with geriatric patients. More facilities are adding dementia care as part of their offerings and these patients need a high level of staff care. If you have an interest in this patient population, spending time in a full-time job at one of these facilities can be very helpful.

Community Service Jobs

There are a number of ways you can give back during your time between college and medical school. Many of my advisees chose to do City Year, a one-year program where they mentored and helped students in secondary school. Others chose to work in positions related to causes they deeply care about such as crisis hotlines or health advocacy groups. Teach for America and Peace Corps are also popular options but require a two-year commitment.

Other Jobs/Activities

Maybe you're a top athlete and want to try to make an Olympic team or you have always dreamed about hiking the Pacific Coast Trail or living abroad. If there is something you are yearning to do, it is best to do it now before starting your medical training. These types of experiences help you learn a lot about how to relate to people with different backgrounds as well as about yourself.

The key with any type of position that does not have a patient care component is to make sure you incorporate a clinical element along the way. For example, add in some shadowing/hospital volunteering on weekends or evenings. This is especially important if you did not gain much clinical experience during college. Medical schools like to see that you are staying connected to patient care while you are engaging in other opportunities.

I hope you are getting the sense that there is no "one size fits all" timeline and you need to be strategic about which one will enable you to be at your strongest point when you apply to medical school. Medical schools will be there when you are ready. If you have a dream or bucket list item you really want to complete, do it.

CHAPTER FIVE

PRE-MED PATHWAY & TIMELINES FOR CAREER-CHANGERS (POST-BACCALAUREATE STUDENTS)

Whether you took time to serve in the Peace Corps or went to work full-time after college and then found yourself thinking about becoming a doctor, you are not alone. Now, there are a significant amount of applicants and matriculants to medical school who are not doing so right after college. According to the Association of American Medical Colleges, the average age of incoming medical students is 24.[1] While the 99th percentile for age of incoming students is 38, some students beyond that age do matriculate as well. Two of my advisees were in their 40s when they applied and were accepted to medical school (both chose osteopathic medicine). Both of them had spouses and children and successfully balanced the demands of the new career they were working towards and their family life.

Generally, your pathway will consist of completing the prerequisite coursework for medical school (either through a formal post-baccalaureate program or by taking the classes a la carte), taking the MCAT, and then applying to medical school. Your timeline for applying will vary based on whether you are taking one or two years to complete the prerequisite coursework.

A caveat for the timelines below: If you are enrolled in a post-baccalaureate program that has a linkage agreement with a medical school and you apply through that, there is a chance you would be able to matriculate to medical school the summer immediately after completing your program. An overview of post-bac programs and linkage agreements appears later in this chapter.

Application timeline if you complete prerequisite coursework in one year:

For the following sample timeline, this career changer plans to finish coursework by May 2020 and plans to matriculate to medical school in August 2021:

Fall 2019 - May 2020	Complete prerequisite coursework (some may opt to start coursework in Summer 2019 and continue through Summer 2020)
Fall 2019/Spring 2020	Complete Committee process if your post-bac program offers a Committee letter; if you plan to apply to a linkage program, work closely with your post-bac program advisor (more on this after the timelines); request letters of recommendation
May 2020	American Medical College Application Service (AMCAS) opens; create your account and begin working on it

June 2020	First chance to submit AMCAS; they will then double-check courses against what you entered and will calculate your GPA. You should also plan to take the MCAT no later than the end of June.
June - August 2020	Complete and submit secondary applications
Fall 2020 to End of March 2021	Interview season
April 30th, 2021	Deadline to decide which one acceptance you want to keep
July/August 2021	Start medical school

Application timeline if you complete prerequisite coursework in two years:

For the following sample timeline, this career changer plans to finish coursework by May 2021 and plans to matriculate to medical school in July/August 2022:

Fall 2019 - May 2021	Complete prerequisite coursework (some may opt to start coursework in Summer 2019 and continue through Summer 2020)
Fall 2020/Spring 2021	Complete Committee process if your post-bac program offers a Committee letter; if you plan to apply to a linkage program, work closely with your post-bac program advisor (more on this after the timelines); request letters of recommendation
May 2021	American Medical College Application Service (AMCAS) opens; create your account and begin working on it

June 2021	First chance to submit AMCAS; they will then double-check courses against what you entered and will calculate your GPA. You should also plan to take the MCAT no later than the end of June.
June - August 2021	Complete and submit secondary applications
Fall 2021 to End of March 2022	Interview season
April 30th, 2022	Deadline to decide which one acceptance you want to keep
July/August 2022	Start medical school

Tips for Career Changers

Consider taking a class or two before applying to a career-changer post-baccalaureate program.

If you have been out of school for a few years, it is good to dip your toe back in that water before diving into a full-time post-baccalaureate program. Taking something like Calculus I might be helpful since Physics classes are often Calculus-based. You could also consider taking an introductory science class.

Carefully research career-changer post-bac programs before applying to them.

There are now well over 100 different programs for students like you who are seeking to complete your prerequisite coursework for medical school. They vary in terms of the program timeframe, curriculum, MCAT prep, advising support, and other factors. Many are full-time and pack all of the prerequisites into one year (usually, you take Gen. Chem. 1 and 2 in the summer and then Organic Chemistry/Biochemistry, Physics, and Biology during the fall and spring). Others are flexible in terms of timing and can be completed in 2 years. Some programs have you take coursework alongside undergraduates whereas in others, courses only have post-bac students in them. Tuition and fees also vary significantly from program to program. These are all factors to take into consideration as you assess the programs that may be right for you.

If attending a full-time post-bac program isn't a viable option for you, consider building your own program by taking all of the prerequisite classes as a non-degree seeking student at a local college/university. I have also had advisees who took jobs at colleges/universities since the employee benefits often include a certain number of classes for free every year. If finances are an issue, then sometimes you may need to explore other creative options for completing the necessary coursework before applying to medical school.

Gain some medically related and volunteer experience prior to applying as well as during the program.

When applying to a career changer program, the admissions committee may want to see evidence that you have explored the medical profession and have a firm sense of why you want to do their program. If clinical experience isn't as emphasized in their admissions process, then they will likely want to see that you have been involved in your community through service. Taking these steps will help you be more certain that medical school is right for you and will make you a more competitive applicant for post-bac programs and medical school.

If you attend a post-bac program that has linkage agreements, consider whether you want to apply to medical school via that pathway.

Career changer post-bac programs often have agreements with specific medical schools in which students can be considered while they are completing their coursework. If you are accepted, you would then be able to matriculate to medical school right after completing your program rather than having a year when you are applying. Programs tend to only let you apply to one linkage school and by doing so, you are indicating your commitment to attend if you are selected for admission. Not all post-bac students choose this option. For example, the Goucher College Post-bac Pre-med Program website states: "In a typical year, approximately one-third of the class will opt to apply to one of our linkage schools.[2] It is very important that you speak with your advisor in the post-bac program to see what your options are and whether you should consider this.

When you apply to medical school, make sure to emphasize your unique experiences and the skills you gained from them.

Your non-linear path to medicine and your life experiences are strengths. Maybe you studied unusual foreign languages, or completed the Peace Corps, or created your own gourmet cookie company, or were a professional athlete. Tell your story in a powerful way in both your written application materials and your interviews.

PART II

HOW TO BECOME A

COMPETITIVE APPLICANT

· CHAPTER SIX ·

HOW MEDICAL SCHOOLS
WILL ASSESS YOU

"I just don't know what medical schools are looking for!" This is a statement I have heard many pre-meds say and it isn't true. The reality is that medical schools have given us a lot of information about what they want to see in applicants' backgrounds. What students are often frustrated by is that there isn't a specific formula of a certain GPA, MCAT score, number of hours of different experiences, and other factors that they can exactly replicate and be guaranteed admission to medical school. In her excellent book *Body of Work*, author Pamela Slim addresses the fact that while everyone is looking for the career hack or formula, it doesn't exist: "Viewing your life as a body of work is not a short-term game. You want to focus on meaning, skill development, professional network development, craft and mastery. There is no one right answer for everyone."[1] With this in mind, let's explore what medical schools look for in applicants and how to begin building a body of work that is uniquely yours.

Core Competencies

The Association of American Medical Colleges recognized a need to develop a clearly defined group of characteristics medical schools would look for as they assessed applicants. They noted: "In order for the admissions community to guide prospective students, the medical education community must first agree upon a set of core competencies before it can develop any tools to assess them. This is not to suggest that some schools will not require or desire competencies in addition to this core set, but this set must be meant to communicate the standard expected of all prospective students."[2] At the end of a long-term process that included the hard work of multiple committees, the AAMC decided on the following 15 core competencies in three main areas[3]:

Pre-Professional Competencies

- Service Orientation

- Social Skills

- Cultural Competence

- Teamwork

- Oral Communication

- Ethical Responsibility to Self and Others

- Reliability and Dependability

- Resilience and Adaptability

- Capacity for Improvement

Thinking & Reasoning Competencies

- Critical Thinking

- Quantitative Reasoning

- Scientific Inquiry

- Written Communication

Science Competencies

- Living Systems

- Human Behavior

There are numerous ways for you to develop these competencies and be able to demonstrate how you did so through different experiences. We will look at the broad areas of experience including academics, research, clinical, community service, and other activities. The AAMC has also developed a part of their website called "Anatomy of an Applicant" that contains print and digital resources including a section on Real Stories Demonstrating Core Competencies as well as a Self-Assessment downloadable guide.[4] Being able to evaluate where you stand in terms of the core competencies will help you determine whether you are ready to apply or if you need more time to strengthen your background.

When reviewing your application, medical schools will look at your Work/Activities section as well as your personal statement to see what types of experiences you have gained and what you have learned from them. They will also look at your letters of recommendation to see how your letter writers articulate ways you demonstrate the core competencies. If you are invited to interview, medical schools will also ask you questions about your experiences. The most competitive applicants generally have done research, gained clinical experience, gotten involved in their community, and pursued interests.

Questions Medical Schools Ask As They Review Applications

At their core, medical school admissions staff are evidence-based and data-driven. They don't work off of your potential or how well you did in high school. Instead, they are looking at your performance from college onwards and whether evidence is there to predict future success. If that evidence is missing, that is a red flag and you have to work to address it before you apply. If you put yourself in their shoes and imagine reviewing over 8,000 applications for an incoming class of maybe 150 students, you understand why they need to see evidence rather than promise.

As medical school admissions committees evaluate you, especially as they decide which applicants to interview, they look for answers to the following questions:

1. Is there ample evidence based on this applicant's academic record that they can excel academically in a rigorous medical school curriculum?

This is a critical factor when your application is reviewed to determine whether you will receive an interview. Unlike colleges which assume a certain percentage of their students will not graduate, medical schools have a virtually 100% graduation rate. They will not interview any applicant who they have concerns about whether they can cut it academically. This reality is reflected in both the national and school specific data.

While a single low grade is not likely to exclude you from consideration, a pattern of low grades, especially in science courses, is problematic. With thousands of applicants to choose from, medical schools have the luxury of only interviewing candidates they feel can do well academically at their particular school. If there are any concerns at all about your academic record, you will likely not be granted an interview.

2. **Did this applicant perform well on the MCAT (both overall and in each section)?**

Since all applicants take the MCAT, it is a standard way to measure knowledge across people's different college/university educational experiences. Additionally, medical schools consider your ability to do well on standardized tests like the MCAT as a predictor of your ability to do so in the future on licensure exams. Since the debut of the new MCAT in 2015, medical schools have been tracking the performance of students on Step One of the United States Medical Licensing Exam (USMLE) compared to their performance on the MCAT. They know exactly what MCAT score correlates with strong performance on Step One and look at applications accordingly.

The new MCAT exam has questions that test your science knowledge, critical reading and analysis skills, and your understanding of psychology/sociology. You need to have both an overall score in line with the average for the medical schools you are applying for as well as consistent scores across each of the four sections.

A high overall score but with lopsided section scores is problematic and you may need to retake it. Remember that your goal is becoming the most competitive applicant possible and if your scores aren't where they need to be, you need to fix this weakness before you apply. No matter how strong your research, clinical, and other experiences may be, if your academic record and/or MCAT scores raise negative questions, you will not move to the interview phase of the application process.

3. Does this applicant have strong letters of recommendation from 4-6 people showing that all of these people have confidence the applicant will thrive in medical school and as a physician?

Many applicants downplay the importance of letters of recommendation but they are actually very important in the process. Medical schools want to see letters from faculty, especially those who taught you in science courses, that show they feel you can excel in a rigorous science-heavy curriculum. They also look for non-academic letters of recommendation, where they can hear from other people you have interacted with in different settings.

4. Is this applicant a good fit for our school?

Each medical school has their own mission statement and personality. When they review your application, they are looking to see if you have the kind of qualities and experiences that will enable you to be a good fit within their particular academic medical community. They will especially be assessing you in this area during your interview.

If you make it through the first round of application review and are invited to interview, the focus will then shift to how you present yourself in person. Are you the same or better in person than you were on paper? Do you exhibit the self-awareness and ability to reflect on your experiences and articulate them effectively? Your interviewers themselves have specific questions in mind and we discuss this topic in the Interviewing chapter.

So, while there isn't a set-in-stone formula to follow as you work towards becoming a competitive applicant, medical schools have given ample information about what they are looking for. Rather than bemoaning the fact there isn't a checklist, embrace the fact that you can chart your own course towards becoming a physician but within a defined framework. We will discuss this further in the next few chapters but the bottom line is you have the freedom to engage in experiences that are meaningful to you and that also help you have a body of work medical schools will value.

CHAPTER SEVEN

WHY YOUR MINDSET & RELATIONSHIPS MATTER

Everything you do builds a foundation that you will need to progress to the next level successfully.

Throughout the next several chapters, we will be giving you tips on academics, experiences, and other important areas you need to develop. Before we do that, it's important to look at the mental side of this process as well as building the meaningful relationships needed.

Create The Right Mindset

The attitude you need to have with all of the different types of experiences (research, clinical, service, and other activities) is to see how interconnected they are and that you will not be able to succeed in more advanced areas if you do not grasp the fundamentals. For example, if you do not master the basics of chemistry, you will not be able to excel in upper-level courses. If you do not learn essential lab techniques, you will not be able to complete more advanced research projects at a high level.

Whatever timeline you are considering for applying to medical school, you need to make sure that in your first two years of college you are doing everything possible to create a solid base of knowledge and experiences. Otherwise, when you get to junior and senior year, you will be on shaky ground instead of on a strong foundation. Train yourself to focus on the long game rather than having a short-term mentality.

Document your experiences along the way.

As a pre-med, it is important to capture interesting experiences and your thoughts and feelings about them and it's best to do so while they are fresh in your mind. Use whatever method works best for you. Some people keep a journal or blog but if you don't plan to carry a notebook with you, there is another option that I call the Shoebox Method. Get a shoebox or container of any kind and put it in a visible place in your room. Some of my previous students have decorated their shoebox with medical imagery like a red cross or the caduceus. When you have experiences, you write them down on whatever paper you have around, even a napkin. Write a brief note about what the experience was and why it was significant to you and also add a date.

Here is a sample entry:

> 4/16/19 - I was shadowing Dr. Smith and observed surgery for the first time. The technology they used was fascinating and I liked seeing all of the different phases of the surgery.

Then, once you get back to your room, put the note in the shoebox. You could create a digital shoebox instead using Google docs, an app on your phone, or another method.

No matter what method you use, when you need to write and speak about your experiences, you can sift through the shoebox and recall events that were meaningful to you. Having a record of your significant and impactful experiences is very helpful when you write your personal statement for applying to medical school. One student brought his shoebox in and we sorted through all of his notes and picked a few key anecdotes. He then used them to create an excellent personal statement.

Create a balance so that you are getting the most out of your college experience while also positioning yourself well for your future career in medicine.

What do you hope to do during college besides getting ready to apply to and hopefully gain admission to medical school? Have you always dreamed of studying abroad? Playing a varsity sport all four years? What else really matters to you? Medical schools will be there whenever you are ready to apply but what won't be there is the ability to go back in time and change your college experience. I have talked to many seniors as they get ready to graduate and the insights they shared are fascinating. Some express regret about what they didn't do while others talk about how happy they are that they stayed true to what they wanted their college experience to be. Then there are the students who share that they had several goals for college but then also remained open to different experiences that came their way. For example, one student was invited by a friend to join the African Drumming Ensemble and this led to developing an interest in African music, completing a study abroad program, and additional experiences that were unplanned but greatly enriched the student's life. You should plan your timeline so that it reflects what you want to get out of your college experience while also working towards getting ready to apply for medical school.

WORK WITH YOUR PRE-MED ADVISOR

You will likely have access to an advisor who has specialized knowledge of the medical school admissions process. Since s/he also often advises on health professions beyond medicine, your advisor may have a title such as Director of Health Professions Advising or Pre-Health Advisor rather than Pre-Med Advisor. At some schools, the advisor is a faculty member or group of faculty members and at others, the advisor is a full-time professional staff member. Larger schools often have a team of health professions advisors. Throughout this book, I refer to these advisors as pre-med or pre-health advisors but it is helpful for you to know that their title on your campus may differ.

Most pre-health advisors belong to an organization called the National Association of Advisors for the Health Professions (NAAHP) and often also belong to one of the four regional associations as well. The National Association of Advisors for the Health Professions "serves as a resource for the professional development of health professions advisors. It is a representative voice with health professions schools and their professional associations, undergraduate institutions, and other health professions organizations. The Association promotes high standards for health professions advising at universities and colleges. It assists advisors in fostering the intellectual, personal, and humanistic development of students as they prepare for careers in health professions."[1]

Advisors participate in ongoing professional development including attending conferences and webinars, communicating with medical school deans, touring medical schools, connecting with each other, and use additional methods to keep their knowledge as current as possible. Advisors also run reports and compile data on applicants and matriculants from their school. Having had the honor of getting to know the advisors at many other schools, I can safely say that advisors are truly passionate about working with students and alumni seeking to become physicians. It is in your best interest to get to know and work with your advisor.

Find out how pre-med advising is structured at your school.

As noted above, each school varies in terms of who does pre-med advising on campus. Many schools have a dedicated person or office that handles pre-med advising whereas others have it done by faculty. In your first semester, go on your school's website and identify who the advisor(s) are at your school. If you notice that the pre-med advisor(s) is presenting a session during Orientation, make sure to attend the event.

Connect with your pre-med advisor early on in your college career.

Meeting your advisor, getting on their email listserv, and being granted access to any resources starting in your freshman year is a very good idea. You can start to establish a good working relationship and learn the details about the opportunities your school provides in terms of research, clinical, and other experiences. Also, your advisor can facilitate connections with pre-meds on campus, alumni physicians, and other key contacts who might be able to serve as mentors.

Some schools may not offer one-on-one advising appointments to students early on in their college careers. If there is group advising or advising by peer mentors, it is worth going so that you can learn more about the path to medical school. Speaking with peer mentors may give you insight into their experiences as pre-meds at your school.

Go to events sponsored by the pre-med advising office and academic departments.

Most pre-med advisors coordinate information sessions with medical school deans, panels with alumni and other physician speakers, field trips, and a wide range of other events. You should plan to attend these events and meet the speakers if possible. You can learn a lot from them and they can even result in future opportunities. For example, one of my former students came to a panel event and had a conversation with one of the pediatricians who spoke. This later resulted in her getting to shadow that physician and even to a clinical research opportunity.

Treat your pre-med advisor and pre-med office staff members professionally.

Pre-med advisors are committed to helping you work towards your goal of gaining admission to medical school but keep in mind that they are working hard to meet the needs of all of their advisees. It is typical for a pre-med advisor to be working with anywhere from 250 to 400 students at any given time and at large universities, the number of pre-meds for any one advisor is even higher. Advisors understand that you are often stressed and have questions but they are not able to be accessible to you 24/7. Like you, advisors also need time to rest and recharge their batteries so that they can be at their best to assist you. Avoid emailing your advisor at 2 am and 6 am and then calling the office at 8:30 am to express your strong annoyance that the advisor has not yet replied to the emails. Professionalism is a very important quality to have in medicine. It is good to start practicing it now as you work with your pre-med advisor.

Learn about whether your school composes a committee letter for applicants and what the process is to get one.

An article in the Association of American Medical Colleges' Advisor Corner defines a committee letter as "a letter authored by a pre-health committee or pre-health advisor and offers evaluation and advocacy on your behalf by highlighting your background and accomplishments, contextualizing challenges, and outlining your overall preparation and motivation for pursuing a career in medicine."[2] Other schools offer a composite letter, where they take quotes from different letters of recommendation and compile them into one document along with sharing some other perspectives on the applicant. A third option is for schools to collect your letters of recommendation and upload them for you. Finally, there are schools that do not compose a committee letter or composite letter or handle any of your recommendation letters. If this is the case for your school, medical schools will understand and not expect a committee letter.

If your school does offer a committee letter, it is important to understand how their committee letter process works. For both of the schools where I worked (Johns Hopkins and Franklin & Marshall College), there was an application that needed to be completed and submitted in early spring. I then held individual interviews to discuss the application, recommendation letters, MCAT timing, and other details. Generally, a faculty committee meets and discusses applicants and then the pre-health advisor or a committee member writes the committee letter based on that feedback. Contact the pre-med advising office to see what the steps are and what deadlines you need to meet. You also need to know whether your school has a GPA cutoff for committee letters. This is another aspect of the process that varies school to school.

GET TO KNOW FACULTY MEMBERS

Speak with professors outside of class and develop good relationships with them.

A student and I met to discuss their plans to apply during the upcoming application cycle. He had an extremely high GPA and solid MCAT score. I shifted gears and asked him to tell me whom he was considering asking for letters of recommendation. He said that because he had done very well in all of his courses, he never attended professors' office hours and didn't know them outside of class. The only people he thought could write a letter was his research mentor and a physician he had shadowed.

Get to know your professors and others both in and beyond the campus community. This will dramatically enrich your college experience and allow you to form working relationships with brilliant scholars who are dedicated to their academic subject. They will inspire you and connecting with them outside of the classroom may point you towards new topics and resources to read and learn about.

There is another reason why these relationships matter: letters of recommendation. When reading letters of recommendation, medical schools want to see that the person knows you on a deeper level and can provide real and helpful insight into who you are and whether you would be a good physician. Some medical schools require two letters of recommendation from professors who taught you in a science course. In these letters, they are looking to see whether that professor feels confident in your aptitude as a student in the sciences and their opinion on whether you could do well in medical school.

In other recommendation letters, schools want to see the perspectives of people who know you in different contexts such as research, clinical experience, volunteering, or other activities. Strong recommendation letters can definitely be helpful and at their core, they are only possible if you cultivate good relationships with people.

FIND MENTORS

Having people in your life who provide guidance and support outside of the academic context is incredibly beneficial. Alumni are often great mentors because they were once in your shoes and are able to share how they got from where you are today to their career in medicine. You can usually look up the contact information for alumni using databases via the Career Services or Alumni Affairs Office at your school. A number of schools offer formal mentoring programs so this is worth looking into as well.

Mentors don't just have to be related to medicine. In fact, you may find you have mentors for specific topics. For example, maybe you sing in a community choir, and the choir director becomes your musical/artistic mentor. Or, perhaps you are training for your first marathon and a local runner becomes a mentor for you. Some people opt to think about their mentors as more of an advisory board and that's fine too. The point is to have people in your corner who you can learn from and who encourage you.

GET TO KNOW MEMBERS OF THE COMMUNITY

Throughout your medical training and work as a physician, you will connect with people from many different backgrounds and walks of life. As Dr. Kirby mentioned earlier, cultivating your communication skills is very important. An excellent way to do this is to find opportunities to develop relationships with people in your community. While it is tempting to stay in the campus bubble and not venture out, your life will be enriched by moving beyond the boundaries of your daily routines.

There are so many different ways to connect with community members. The most obvious is through service opportunities. This may seem intimidating from a time standpoint but you can actually seek out chances to volunteer to help with specific events such as charity run/walks, student mentoring days, and others. Elderly care facilities are often looking for students to come have conversations with residents and keep them engaged. It is remarkable hearing other peoples' stories and their insights about the different times they have lived through and changes they have witnessed. You will likely find that these types of conversations expand the way you think about medicine, the world more broadly, and yourself.

For both mindset and relationships, no one will do this for you. It is up to you to see the value in them and make them a priority. It will not be a "one and done" situation; rather, both need to be tended to and nurtured on a consistent basis. Ultimately, they will make you a better doctor.

CHAPTER EIGHT

ACADEMICS

Your academic preparation is one of the most important aspects of your application, not to mention making sure you are ready to excel in medical school. Creating an action plan at the beginning of college is time well spent. You can begin mapping out how you will complete your major(s) as well as the prerequisite courses for medical school. If you're not sure what you might major in (since many schools have you declare in the spring of your sophomore year), you can create several different possible plans. This is where your academic and/or pre-health advisor can be very helpful. You can continue to revisit and refine the plan before course registration for the next semester.

Learn what the prerequisite courses are for medical school and think about where they will fit in your academic plans.

Each medical school has the ability to decide what prerequisite courses they require. While there are some shifts going on at individual schools, the majority of medical schools require the following courses:

- A year of General Chemistry with labs

- A year of Organic Chemistry with labs

  – Some medical schools have shifted to requiring 1 semester with lab instead

- A year of General Biology with labs

- A semester of Biochemistry

- A year of Physics with labs

- A year of Math

  – Type of math varies; often Calculus and/or Statistics

- Coursework focused on writing/humanities and behavioral sciences (psychology, sociology)

  – Most medical schools require two semesters of writing-intensive coursework

  – With the addition of psychology and sociology content on the MCAT, some schools have now added these to their requirements

If you have a particular dream school in mind, it is worth looking at their Admissions website to see what their prerequisites are and if they have any other courses that they strongly recommend.

Understand that there may be a difference between how your college or university structures specific classes versus what medical schools require.

Each college or university gets to decide how they structure their courses both in terms of credit and content. For example, some colleges and universities have science course credits as combined lecture and lab (let's say that is 4 credits) whereas others have the lecture and lab separately (a 3 credit lecture, a 1 credit lab). For a course like Biochemistry, if your school has that as a combined lecture and lab course, that's how you will complete it regardless of the fact the lab may not be required by medical schools. Another example is Physics. At some colleges and universities, they have Calculus I and II as co-requisites for taking Physics I and II whereas other schools may just require Calculus I and then you could just take Statistics as your other math class. A third example is Biology. At some colleges and universities, their introductory Biology sequence is three courses instead of two and you have to take all three to be able to take Biochemistry. I think you are seeing that your path to completing the medical school prerequisites varies a lot based on your particular college or university and this is where your pre-med advisor comes in.

Do not overload on science classes during your first semester.

I remember meeting with a sophomore for the first time and in looking at her transcript before our appointment, I saw that she had decided to take Calculus, Physics, and Chemistry during their first semester. She failed Chemistry and got C and D grades in the other sciences. When I asked her why she chose to take these courses together, she said she just wanted to get through all of the prerequisites for medical school as fast as possible.

Repeat: THIS IS A MARATHON, NOT A SPRINT! No medical school will be impressed that you overloaded, especially in your first semester, and that you tried to get your prerequisite courses done as quickly as possible. Doing poorly in prerequisite courses hurts you on many levels. Also, taking too many of these classes early means that when you are studying for the MCAT later on, you may end up having to re-teach yourself a lot of the information.

Be careful about using AP classes to place out of introductory courses.

One student I met with came into college with AP credits in all of the sciences. Against advice, he decided to place out of introductory chemistry and biology and took Organic Chemistry and an upper-level biology class during his first semester. What he didn't realize was that the other students in these classes were sophomores and others who had all already adjusted to academics at the college level. He struggled through and ended up with Cs in both science classes.

In general, it is not wise to use AP credit to place out of introductory science courses. It is far better to take those classes at your college or university to get the proper foundation you need for upper-level science classes and hopefully earn good grades along the way. AP credits are great for applying to college but not very useful when applying to medical school. Most medical schools require upper-level coursework in any subject in which you try to use AP credit to place out so again, you can really shoot yourself in the foot by relying on APs. Some colleges and universities do allow you to get some academic credit for AP classes without causing you to place out of science courses. You can ask the Registrar's office or your academic advisor about your school's policy.

Consider starting with introductory foreign language courses in college, even if you took them in high school.

A freshman who had taken Spanish during all 4 years of high school decided to take an advanced Spanish class their first semester. We met mid-way through the semester and she said that they felt the pace of the class was significantly faster and more in depth than high school and she felt overwhelmed by it. Also, she said a lot of her classmates were Spanish majors who had already taken at least two years of the language in college. She ended up deciding to withdraw from the class.

Why not start at the beginning with a 100 level course? Yes, you have covered that material in your years of studying the language in high school but it is good to gain the fundamentals again in college. This often means that you can do well and not have to devote as many hours to this subject as you would if you took an advanced class. This can be helpful in terms of allocating your studying time effectively while balancing the demands of lab-based courses.

Choose a major that is a good fit for your skills and interests.

One student decided to major in Biology because she told me that everyone said that was what she had to do in order to go to medical school. Many of the upper-level classes ended up being more focused on plant biology, a subject she was less interested in. She ended up not doing as well in those classes and even though she had done well in her prerequisites for medical school, those additional Biology courses for her major brought down both her science and cumulative GPA.

An almost identical situation happened with another student. He chose to major in Chemistry and although he did well in the introductory courses as well as the more applied courses such as Biochemistry, the more math-heavy chemistry courses like Physical Chemistry were very hard for him. Again, the end result was his GPA took a big hit.

Choose a major you enjoy and in which you can excel. If you choose something you think you "have to do to be able to go to medical school" but is a subject you don't enjoy, you won't study it as much or connect with the material in a way that enables you to do well in the courses. There is no one major that medical schools look for and every year, thousands of applicants with majors in many subjects literally from A to Z (anthropology to zoology) gain admission to medical school. The caveat for this is if you are an international student. Due to the terms of your student visa (specifically the Curricular Practical Training portion), you can only engage in summer activities directly tied to your major. This means you have to be more strategic in your choice of major. I describe this in more depth in Advice for International Students chapter.

Take humanities courses.

Classes in subjects like religious studies, women/gender and

LGBTQ studies, racial/ethnic studies, and other areas will raise your awareness of issues unique to different patient populations. There are probably issues you have never considered but for people from diverse racial, gender identity, and religious backgrounds, they encounter challenges every day. Hearing from your fellow students about their life experiences can also be helpful.

Humanities courses also train you to think in a different way as well as to write effectively. Some students who are excellent in the sciences struggle with writing but with hard work, can improve their skills dramatically. Being able to express yourself clearly in writing is important in medicine and by taking humanities classes, you are better preparing yourself for your future career.

Think about studying abroad.

Many students dream about spending a semester studying abroad but are worried that as pre-meds, it won't be possible. I am happy to share that not only is it possible but it can be a life-changing, career-affirming experience. Many of my advisees chose to complete medically related programs such as the Health & Society Program at King's College London, the Medical Practice & Policy and Public Health Programs through DIS in Copenhagen and Stockholm, and many others (I am not endorsing any particular program but am sharing what previous students did). I have also had students choose programs that were not health-related, such as studying abroad in Italy to focus on art or studying abroad in Paris to immerse themselves in French language and culture. Some students, including those participating in varsity sports, found that it was easier to spend a portion of a summer studying abroad rather than being away from campus for a whole semester.

When you decide whether you want to study abroad and if so, when you plan to go, you then need to make sure to plan your coursework accordingly. It's not a good idea to try to complete medical school prerequisite coursework abroad for multiple reasons. First, schools abroad structure their courses and exams very differently from colleges/universities here. For example, in the U.K., your grades in many courses are largely decided by one substantial exam at the end of the term. For subjects like science and math, you really need to know how you are doing along the way. Second, not all medical schools might accept the coursework as fulfilling the prerequisite.

Work closely with your college/university's Study Abroad office to discuss questions about timing, program options, and other matters specific to how your school handles international study. You also need to consult with your school's pre-health advisor about how studying abroad will fit into your plans and when you want to apply to medical school. If it is something you have always wanted to do, go for it!

If you are considering a double major, really reflect on whether that is right for you.

A student had decided to double major in Biochemistry and Music because her mother told her that would look good to medical schools. Having to balance a significant amount of time in lab-based classes with a lot of hours of music practice/rehearsals was difficult plus the Music major requirements also included theory and composition classes. The student shared that she felt that all she ever did was biology and music. She envied their friends who were taking classes in other subjects. Also, she had to overload on courses (taking 5 rather than 4 in several semesters) in order to complete the requirements for both majors. She ended up struggling academically and not achieving at the level she needed to in order to be a competitive applicant.

Majoring in one subject is fine. Medical schools do not place more value on a double major nor do they expect it. Often, choosing a major in one subject and completing a minor in another is a more manageable choice that still allows you to study subjects in more depth. Completing a double major but having a lower GPA will not help your chances of getting accepted to medical school.

Don't succumb to FOBB (the Fear of Being Behind).

Think about FOBB as a cousin of FOMO. Neither one is helpful in your life! There are so many different combinations and ways you can take the courses you need to fulfill the prerequisites for medical school. Also, there is not only one timeline for everyone. There is just whatever timeline ends up being right for you.

When choosing courses, consider the source of your advice (peers vs. professors and advisors).

I was meeting with a student who told me that their House Adviser, a senior pre-med, told him that he had to take specific courses his first semester or he would be really behind. This was completely untrue. Once I explained course-sequencing options to the student, and when he could take the different prerequisite courses, he felt relieved.

Another student came in and asked about summer courses. Apparently, a friend of hers told her that she could just take all of the prerequisites for medical school over the summer at a college close to home and that the classes would be easier there. Again, this is not good advice. When the student and I discussed how medical schools would perceive this negatively, we talked about several ways she could take the prerequisites and she left feeling more confident about her options.

Even though other students have good intentions, they are speaking from very limited experience and their academic background may be very different from yours. Seek academic advice from advisors and professors who have extensive knowledge of the pre-med requirements and who have successfully helped many students gain admission to medical school. If your pre-major advisor is not as knowledgeable in terms of what courses you should be taking, make sure to consult with your pre-med advisor and other faculty members as needed.

Prioritize your academics over extracurricular activities.

I met with a student who presented me with what he called his resume, which was actually a ten-page list of all of the clubs and activities he had participated in during college. When I saw that his GPA was well below a 3.0, I asked him why he chose to be involved in so many clubs. He said that he enjoyed them and also figured they would help him be a better applicant for medical school. I explained that if medical schools had any concerns about his ability to do well in their curriculum, they would not move forward with considering him, no matter how long or impressive his list of activities was.

You are a student first and everything else is second. Do not allow extracurricular activities to invade the time needed to study effectively and do well academically. In terms of activities, choose quality over quantity and do not take on more than you can handle. My wonderful former colleague Kathy called it the Panera approach: You Pick Two. Start with only a few activities in your first year of college. You can always add more in once you have adjusted to the academic workload and college life.

For some students, this is a really hard transition to make because in high school, they were able to do a lot of activities as well as earn top grades. The reality is that college level academics are harder and go more in depth than high school courses. As a result, the amount of studying needed to do well in a course is much more than it was in high school. During your first year in college, start small in terms of club involvement. You can always build in more after you have gotten your confidence academically in college.

Learn how to learn, how you specifically learn, and how to study effectively.

I have had this conversation so many times with students. When they would say they weren't doing well in a particular class, such as Organic Chemistry, I would ask them to tell me how they studied for their last exam. One young man said that he had worked really hard and studied for at least 3 hours a day in the two days leading up to the exam. A young woman said that she had re-read her notes many times for at least two weeks. Both of these study methods had fallen short and neither student had earned a good grade on their exam.

You need to learn how to learn. In high school, you may have gotten by on just memorizing and regurgitating information but in college, you will have to memorize and also synthesize information to apply it to new questions. It is essential to engage in more active forms of studying such as using flashcards to test yourself, completing a number of practice problems, and even drawing pictures or diagrams of what you are learning. Also, treat science as a foreign language and study it consistently every day. That way, when a test comes around, you have learned the material at a deep level and can apply it to the problems you are asked to solve.

Try not to work too many hours at an on or off-campus job.

A student and I were discussing their academic performance since it was clear by looking at her transcript that she was struggling. She admitted she was working at least 20 hours a week and then full-time during breaks in order to help defray the cost of tuition and other expenses. She ended up needing to complete a special Master's program to improve her academic record. Making the conscious decision not to work during that program paid off, since she earned outstanding grades and was then accepted to medical school.

Money is a sensitive subject and I am well aware of the rising costs of college tuition. The reality is that if you have to work a substantial number of hours to cover costs and that hurts your academic performance, then it isn't worth sacrificing your study time. Consider having a conversation with the financial aid office to explore different options you might have. If you do need to have a campus job, consider getting one that would give you time to study while working. Also, during the summer, you may be able to work and save up a chunk of money you can then tap into during the academic year. This strategy has worked well for many of my advisees.

Plan to complete your prerequisite courses for medical school during the academic year rather than the summer (if possible).

Over the years, I have had many students ask about whether they could use their summers to complete courses required by medical schools. They often wanted to take these courses back home and the level of rigor at those other schools may or may not have been comparable to their college or university. Summers are best used to gain research, clinical, or other experiences. Medical schools strongly prefer to see coursework taken during the academic year at your home institution. Also, some students really struggle with the immersion format of summer courses. You are cramming a course that is usually 12-13 weeks into a 5-week period and as a result, you will be in class every day. If you have a strong reason for needing to take a summer class, for example, you want to study abroad and wouldn't be able to take the class otherwise, then you can consider it. The bottom line is not to plan on taking a significant amount of summer classes. Instead use that time to expand your experiences.

Avoid having a pattern of low grades.

I have seen students successfully overcome having one low grade. For example, a student got a C+ in Organic Chemistry but earned very good grades in all other classes and ended up getting into 4 medical schools. It is much harder to overcome having a pattern of low grades. I met with one student who didn't have any science grades above a B-. I advised that after the student graduated, he could take a class or two as a non-degree seeking student to see whether he had just struggled in science at the school where he went to college or if it was a general challenge with science courses. After doing well in these courses, the student then went on to complete a record-enhancing post-baccalaureate program to further strengthen his science background.

If you find yourself in a position where you already have one low science grade and are struggling in another science class, you may want to consider withdrawing from it and then picking science coursework back up when you are more prepared to do well. This will help you avoid digging a significant hole that will take years to get out of in terms of GPA.

Do not plagiarize or engage in any behavior that would lead to having an institutional action on your record.

On your primary application to medical school, you have to disclose any academic or other kind of misconduct. One student struggled to gain admission because she had been sanctioned for an academic misconduct related to plagiarism. Another student had a pattern of getting into physical fights and this went on his record. This was a concern for medical schools and despite applying to a large number of schools, he did not gain admission.

Your actions are important and bad decisions can haunt you. Do not engage in behavior that would lead anyone to question whether you have the professionalism and character needed to become a doctor. While minor infractions are often not deal breakers in terms of admission to medical school, patterns raise major red flags. Also, academic misconduct, especially cheating on exams or committing major plagiarism, is taken very seriously.

If tragedy strikes, give yourself the time you need to heal and then start moving forward again towards your goal of attending medical school.

While life brings moments of beauty and joy, it can also bring extremely painful experiences. Some of my advisees have had their roommates die tragically while others had parents diagnosed with terminal illnesses who then ultimately lost their battle against the disease. Others faced their own serious health issues that required surgery and recovery time.

If something like this happens to you, be especially kind and compassionate to yourself rather than trying to suppress your feelings. The last thing you want to do is push forward as if everything is perfectly fine and then find yourself crashing physically and/or emotionally at some point in the semester. It is ok to say to yourself, "Hey, right now, things aren't ok and I need some time to process this." You should then work closely with your academic advisor, pre-med advisor, and others to discuss potential options. I have had students who decided to take short-term personal or medical leaves, switch a class from a grade to pass/fail, or temporarily have Incompletes listed on their course record until finishing those courses for grades early in the next semester or during the summer. Also, colleges and universities have Counseling Centers that offer a variety of services. When you are ready, you can pick back up where you left off and continue building the academic and experiential background that will help you get into medical school.

CHAPTER NINE

RESEARCH, CLINICAL, SERVICE, *&* OTHER ACTIVITIES

As we discussed in the chapter on How Medical Schools will Assess You, they want to see evidence that shows you have developed the core competencies that they are looking for. In this chapter, we are going to look at each of the main types of experiences that help you demonstrate the competencies and get the foundation you need to be successful in medical school. Understanding these areas will help you be strategic about which activities to engage in and when to do so.

RESEARCH EXPERIENCE

Your research experience does not have to be medically related (but can be if you want).

What medical schools appreciate about applicants who have research in their background is the set of skills you cultivated as a result of that experience. The specific type of research is less important as the length of time spent, the depth of your experience, and what you learned. I have had successful advisees whose research focused on collecting and analyzing soil samples from local riverbeds, the behavior of birds, bleaching of coral reefs, and plenty of other topics that are not medically related. Find a project that sparks your interest and then really delve into it.

Be able to talk about your research, your role in it, and what you have learned from it.

You should always think about and be able to share what the goal of your research is and how different aspects of the project will contribute to that goal. Also, reflect on the challenges you face and obstacles you overcome. Medical schools like to hear about these types of experiences since they demonstrate your adaptability and resilience.

Begin approaching professors early if you want to do research on campus.

One of my advisees started speaking with a professor about possible research opportunities during spring of her freshman year. She started out as a volunteer in the genetics lab and went on to take independent study research courses and even had a publication in her senior year. Gaining skills and exposure to research early on sets you up well for the rest of your college career.

When assessing possible labs to join, look at the publication track record of the professor as well as students in his/her lab.

Given that you'll likely be devoting a lot of time to research if you join a professor's lab, you want to see the nature of the projects they are working on. Additionally, it is helpful to see whether students in that professor's lab have been able to co-author publications based on their work. There are a few ways you can find out this information. First, most colleges and universities have websites for each academic department, which often have a list of faculty members and their research. Additionally, you can use Google Scholar to look up their publications. Reference librarians on campus can also be very helpful.

If lab research isn't for you, consider clinical research.

Some students dread being in a lab-based research setting since it is often more solitary and can often be tedious. Clinical research can be a good option instead. In this type of research, you are often working directly with patients enrolled in a study as well as the physicians and scientists running the study.

While there are some clinical research internships, often the best option is to create your own opportunity. One way to do this is to use clinicaltrials.gov, which is the listing of all privately and publically funded trials in the world involving human subjects. You can search for a specific disease/condition, a location, or a combination of terms. You can then read about the different studies and see the contact people for them. This isn't an internship database so you will need to reach out to the contact people listed and inquire about whether they would be open to having a research volunteer or intern. One of my advisees got an amazing research opportunity at Yale by using this method and others have obtained research internships at other elite institutions in the U.S. and abroad.

Another way to do this is by using Google Scholar. You can search for different areas you're interested in (for example, pediatric seizures) and then look at the list of authors for the study. Many times, their institutional affiliation is listed and sometimes even their contact information. You can then reach out to them via email to see whether they might take you as an intern or volunteer.

Summer is a great time to gain research experience.

Being able to devote 40+ hours a week for 10-12 weeks over summer enables you to work on a research project with more depth and concentration than you could devote during the academic year. Many academic medical centers have internships listed on their website and you can apply directly. The deadlines are often in January and February so definitely plan ahead! The Association of American Medical Colleges has a list of research internships on their website that is worth browsing.[1]

Also, check with your pre-health advisor to see what opportunities might be available through your school. Some colleges/universities provide funding for students to do full-time research under the guidance of a faculty mentor. Like the deadlines for national programs, school sponsored programs often have deadlines early in the spring semester so definitely make sure you are aware of when applications are due.

If you are considering an MD/PhD, thoroughly consider whether you want your career to have substantial focus on research and plan on making sure you have an exceptional track record in research.

I have worked with many students who were passionate about both research and patient care and were thinking about applying to MD/PhD programs. Becoming a physician scientist is an even longer process than medical school since you will take time in your medical training to complete your PhD. Most physician scientists spend the majority of their time doing research and might see patients a few hours a week. Plenty of MDs assist with research while having their primary focus on practicing medicine.

If you are seriously considering an MD/PhD, then you must have an impressive background in research. Simply volunteering in a lab or doing a low level project won't be enough to convince admissions committees that you have what it takes to complete the PhD portion of the dual degree. While publications aren't required, they can certainly demonstrate a level of proficiency in both research and writing. Consult with your pre-med advisor as well as with faculty members to discuss whether the MD/PhD path is right for you.

CLINICAL EXPERIENCE

Get a combination of shadowing experience and hands-on patient interactions/care.

When you are shadowing physicians, you are essentially a fly on the wall. Shadowing is helpful for gaining insight into the doctor-patient relationship as well as how different doctors collaborate with each other, nurses, physician assistants, and others. It can also enable you to see what different medical specialties are like.

Interacting directly with patients yourself is also very important not only in terms of you becoming a competitive applicant but also to help you decide whether you actually like the reality of medicine. Volunteering at a hospital in a role where you transport patients around, bring them meals, or communicate with them in other ways is a good option. Elderly care facilities are also a good place to interact with patients and can give you insight into geriatric medicine and dementia care.

Another way to gain clinical experience is to become an EMT. Several advisees of mine took the EMT class over the summer and then joined the Emergency Medical Services squad when they got back to campus. Working at an elderly care facility is also a great way to work with patients and is something medical schools appreciate seeing in an application. One dean told me that his admissions committee loves to see that type of experience since caring for elderly patients has become a big part of medicine. Along those lines, becoming a hospice volunteer can be a powerful experience. You will be working with patients facing terminal conditions and who are in the late stages of battling these illnesses. Immersing yourself in what it is really like to work with patients is very important.

Try to shadow physicians in a range of specialties and in different stages of their career.

Since your goal when shadowing is to gain an understanding of the reality of healthcare today as well as see how physicians interact with patients and their colleagues, it is helpful to observe different physicians if possible. Witnessing the day-to-day experience of physicians in areas such as primary care, surgery, emergency medicine, and other areas will give you a much better picture of what being a doctor today is like. It can be interesting to shadow physicians who are completing their residency or fellowship training as well as physicians who are more established in their careers. If you are considering osteopathic medical school, you should definitely plan on shadowing a DO. It will be helpful for you to learn about the osteopathic philosophy and also many osteopathic medical schools now require a letter of recommendation from a DO.

Connect with physicians you may already know, such as your pediatrician.

I have had many students who contacted their pediatrician and were able to arrange chances to shadow them. In other cases, the pediatrician put them in touch with other doctors they were able to observe. If you have relatives or family friends in medicine, you can also touch base with them about shadowing opportunities. Consider contacting staff members at your old high school to see if you can be connected with any physicians who attended that same school. A little creative thinking goes a long way in terms of creating shadowing opportunities.

Speak with your pre-med advisor about school-sponsored opportunities as well as ways to contact alumni physicians.

Many pre-med advising offices coordinate shadowing programs that enable students to gain exposure to medicine. At some colleges and universities, you can complete an internship or class and receive academic credit. At others, the shadowing programs are not for credit but are still very beneficial. Pre-health advisors are in touch with local doctors or have access to the database of all alumni physicians across the country. Make sure to take advantage of these opportunities and resources.

Explore medical professional associations.

Every medical specialty has a professional association that doctors can join. For example, the American Academy of Pediatrics is the organization for pediatricians, the American College of Physicians is for internal medicine doctors and subspecialists, and the American College of Surgeons is for surgeons. When you see letters such as FACP or FACS after a physician's name, it means s/he has been inducted as a Fellow of the American College of Physicians or a Fellow of the American College of Surgeons. Most medical professional associations have chapters at the state level and often have someone designated as a contact person. Additionally, most of the national websites for medical professional associations have "Find a Doctor" searchable databases where you can put in your zip code or city/state and a list of physicians in the area will come up. You could then reach out to these physicians to inquire about opportunities to shadow or volunteer.

Not all of your shadowing or volunteer experience needs to be done with a physician.

One of my advisees volunteered at a local hospital where she spent significant time with the nursing staff in the Emergency Department as well as in the Intensive Care Unit. The nurses allowed the student to be with them during all aspects of their shifts, from caring for patients, to completing documentation, to setting up equipment and more. The nurses also shared their insights into how the healthcare field has evolved and the different roles each person played in the ER or ICU. The student ended up getting an advanced education because of the time she spent with the nursing staff.

Other students who were on the fence between medicine and another health profession did shadowing in both. For example, a student shadowed physicians and dentists and ultimately decided dentistry was a better fit. Gaining insight into diverse healthcare careers and how roles complement each other can be very helpful.

If you do a medical mission trip or other short-term experience, be thoughtful about what you see and experience there and do not do anything you would not be allowed to do here.

Many pre-meds are now spending their spring break or a portion of their summer going to a developing country for a medical mission trip. Some only do these trips because they think medical schools will find them impressive. While some medical schools may view this type of week-long trip as positive, others may see it as "voluntourism" at best and exploitative at worst. They also recognize that now there are many companies organizing these types of trips and that many students can't afford the $6,000 or more that these can cost.

While a medical mission trip can be an interesting experience, there are a few important things to keep in mind. First, these patients deserve just as much respect and care as anyone in the United States. I was horrified when a student told me about his trip and said how cool it was to "play doctor" there and get to do sutures and other procedures on patients. This is wrong on so many levels. Recognize what a privilege it is for you to meet these patients and help them. You should never do anything for which you do not have significant training and that you would not be legally allowed to do here in the United States. Second, if you feel like the trip was a life-changing experience that opened your eyes to health disparities, don't come back home and do nothing. There are patients here who are experiencing similar challenges with gaining access to care. One dean told me about a personal statement an applicant had written about how his two-week medical mission trip to Africa changed his life but there was no evidence that upon coming back to campus, he made any effort to get involved in similar issues locally. Your actions speak louder than your words.

Don't only focus on hours; focus on quality.

A lot of pre-meds ask me how many shadowing hours they need. Unlike physician assistant and other health professions schools, medical schools often don't have a defined number of required hours of shadowing or patient care. Instead of heavily focusing on a specific number, shift your emphasis to getting experiences that help you gain deeper insight into medicine. What medical schools want to see in your application materials and your interview is that you understand the reality of modern medicine and why you want to become a doctor.

Keep notes on what you see.

Earlier, I mentioned the importance of documenting your experiences throughout your time as a pre-med but I want to emphasize how important it is for your clinical experiences. While something seems amazing and memorable today, that memory will fade unless you capture it. One student kept a diary of diseases, where he recorded all of the different medical conditions they observed. This is a great idea and something you could keep adding to in medical school and beyond.

COMMUNITY SERVICE

You need to have service experiences during college, not just high school.

Since so many high schools require community service hours, only having those hours and none during college is not going to help you be a strong candidate. Most medical schools will only consider college hours on your application. Medicine is a service profession so gaining experience in giving back is important.

Get involved in the community off campus.

The campus bubble is a real phenomenon and often students make the mistake of overloading with activities and clubs rather than venturing out into the local community. Make an effort to seek volunteer opportunities in the area. Many colleges/universities have an office devoted to service/volunteering so that is a good place to start.

Volunteer work doesn't have to be medically related.

Find an opportunity that aligns with one of your interests. If you love working with children, consider volunteering at a local school or through a mentoring program like Big Brothers, Big Sisters. If you like working with your hands, think about helping build houses through Habitat for Humanity. Some of my students who were interested in math got trained as volunteer tax preparers and helped low-income residents file their returns. Service is about giving back and also creates a chance for you to build relationships with people from all walks of life and backgrounds that are different from yours.

Don't just do fundraising activities.

While fundraising for nonprofit organizations and charities is great, you are often doing that work on campus or online rather than interacting with the people the funds will benefit. The human component of service is important and can't be experienced in the same way if there is distance between you and people you seek to help. Also, fundraising tends to be a fairly short-term activity rather than an ongoing commitment. Fundraising can be done in conjunction with other more people-facing roles.

Service can be done anywhere, including abroad.

There are many ways to engage in service across the U.S. or internationally. Again, this does not have to be medically related. For example, students go abroad through organizations like Engineers without Borders and work on building wells in rural areas. A good first step is to touch base with your campus office of service and people who coordinate study abroad.

OTHER ACTIVITIES

Choose depth over breadth - fewer clubs/activities but done over a longer period of time.

In terms of activities, what got you into college will not get you into medical school. Medical schools do not want to see an exploding resume featuring tons and tons of clubs that you were only involved in as a member and for only a semester or two. They would prefer seeing a deeper commitment over time. If you have a pattern of shallow, short-term involvement or a ton of activities but a lower GPA, medical schools may not invite you to interview there. If you do get an interview, they may ask pointed questions about your priorities and decision-making skills.

Having progressive levels of leadership within an organization over time is good, if possible. For example, you could start out as a member, then serve on a Committee, and potentially work your way up to a broader leadership role. Depth over breadth also means you are not overloading yourself with commitments outside of the classroom and that you are leaving enough time to devote to studying.

Pursue interests and hobbies.

If there are things you love to do but they don't show up on a transcript or resume, you should still do them. Whether you love to sing or dance, play sports at the varsity or club level, knit, paint, run marathons, build robots, or any other hobby, it is well worth your time to keep pursuing those interests. It can actually make you a better applicant for medical school. Schools want to see that you are a well-rounded person with interests beyond academics and other activities. Sometimes in interviews, you may be speaking with a person who shares your interests and may spend a good deal of time discussing them with you. Also, when schools see that you have an outlet for stress relief and an activity that makes you happy, they consider this as a good sign you can balance academics and life.

·CHAPTER TEN·

DR. KIRBY'S DIAGNOSIS –
ACADEMICS & RESEARCH

The "Nobody Cares" Concept

The Nobody Cares concept developed from my own experiences
and observing other students and people. I noticed that people
would often do things that they think will benefit themselves by
impressing others. This is often done on a perceived benefit that is
usually based on rumors, stories or suggestions rather than facts.
Since it is based on perception instead of reality, the effort to impress
often backfires and the person winds up worse off than before.
Nobody Cares refers to you doing something that you think will
be impressive but the action actually has no positive effect on the
intended target. The person does not care about the thing you are
doing that you think is so important. They are often indifferent or
have a negative reaction.

College is a time when people are particularly vulnerable to this.
Students are suddenly put in the position of making many decisions
about their life. They often rely on the wisdom of their fellow

students to help determine how they act. For the premed student this often results in students doing things to impress medical school admission in an effort to improve their resume or curriculum vitae. Unfortunately, the opposite often happens.

The Nobody Cares concept covers all aspects of your college career. In high school, you have a set curriculum and daily supervision to help ensure your success. In medical school, your career is carefully developed to make sure you succeed since medical schools want everyone they accept to graduate. In college you are largely on your own with limited guidance to help you make good decisions. In this environment it is not uncommon for students to make choices that they think will be very impressive to medical admissions officers that are actually very harmful. This applies to all aspects of college including academics, extracurricular activities, research, and summer jobs.

In academics, the typical mistake is to take on a course load that is very difficult with the idea that the student will get extra consideration for it. Examples include taking upper level courses as a freshman, doing a double major, or taking too many science courses at once. The reality is that nobody in medical school admissions cares if you choose a more difficult course load if you don't do well. The bottom line is that you have to be competitive and choosing an overly ambitious course load can hurt your chances of success.

The same applies to extracurricular activities. Students with marginal grades often think that doing lots of extracurricular activities will compensate for a marginal GPA. Instead of doing extra work to improve their grades, they take time away from their studies to do extracurricular activities. The result is usually that their grades remain the same or even go down. Again, Nobody Cares if you decide to do lots of extracurricular activities if your grades make you non-competitive.

The same concept applies to research and summer jobs. In this area the mistake is to choose a situation that you think will be very impressive on paper but does not actually result in the experience and recommendations that will be helpful. A less impressive-sounding choice may result in a much better learning experience and positive recommendations. Again, it is the positive experience and results that are important, not what you think will look impressive.

In summary, in all aspects of your college career you will make critical decisions that will affect your final resume. Your decisions should be based on research and data, not on what you think will be impressive. Remember, Nobody Cares about extra things you think are impressive, they care about the final grades and resume you present when you apply to medical school.

Academics

Becoming used to utilizing the approach I described earlier, namely learning based on knowledge of fundamentals with increasing levels of complexity, will help prepare you for medical school. Some courses like organic chemistry or languages such as Spanish are ideally suited to this approach. In Spanish there is the basic conjugation of verbs, which is the same for most verbs in the different tenses. There are exceptions that must be memorized. By knowing the basic structures and exceptions, you become able to read and speak Spanish. Similarly, organic chemistry has many basic equations with notable exceptions. By understanding the basic equations and knowing the exceptions you are able to solve more complex equations. In other courses the fundamental principles may not be as obvious but you can use the same approach. For example, in a survey course on religion you can try to determine what fundamental concepts are shared by the religions and what variations make the individual religions unique. Utilizing this approach to your classes will make you well prepared for the sequential learning of medicine.

Another useful approach is to get used to thinking there may be principles that are fundamental to one area, that lend themselves to a better understanding of another field. An example of this is tumor biology and Darwinian evolution. If you look at a cancer as a collection of individual cells within a tumor (group), you can see that tumor growth can be similar to Darwinian evolution. The individual tumor cells that selectively grow as the tumor grows can be cells that exhibit different characteristics like chemotherapy resistance or ability to live with less nutrients or vascular supply. The changing tumor and surrounding tissue will allow for cells with specific attributes to proliferate just like in Darwinian evolution. You may not find many of these connections between courses but having an open mind and looking for shared common themes will make you better prepared to recognize unusual presentations of disease.

I saw an example of this when I was in training. A young child was admitted into the hospital with ascending paralysis. All the diagnostic tests and conventional therapy failed to recognize the cause or effectively treat the disease. The disease progressed to the point where the child was having respiratory difficulty and would soon need intubation. An older physician did a thorough examination of the child's scalp and found a tick, which he removed, and the child walked out of the hospital later that day. Presented with a problem of ascending paralysis of unknown cause, the physician thought of tick-released neurotoxin as a possible cause and was able to cure the child.

Other than these basic learning principles, there are other things you should do and things to avoid in your academic career. If you have made the decision to be a pre-med then from that time forward you should treat your college career as a job with the goal of being promoted to medical school. You need to recognize that making mistakes can hurt or end your chances for career advancement.

You should not place out of introductory courses based on AP credit from high school. If you do, your first course will be in class with students ranging from freshman to seniors, including students who major in that subject. It will be very difficult to compete with the upperclassmen. Remember, you are not only trying to learn, but also to create a GPA that makes you a competitive applicant. Medical schools want to see that you can achieve at a high level because they expect all of their chosen students to become doctors. Taking on an overly ambitious course schedule is an example of bad judgment, not an impressive task.

Develop disciplined, persistent study habits. You may be able to succeed in college by skipping class and cramming before tests but that approach is short sighted. If you commit to a consistent daily/weekly study schedule you can maximize your learning of the topics in a given class. In this way, you are preparing yourself for the large volume of material you will encounter as a medical student. In addition, by thoroughly knowing your subject matter, you can have more in-depth interaction with professors, which can lead to further opportunities for research and recommendations. College is a significant investment of time and money and the sooner you learn to apply yourself, the more benefit you will earn on your investment.

A corollary to consistent study is to learn how you study best. Hopefully you will already have an idea of what works for you from your success in high school. It doesn't matter how your fellow students, family members, or anyone else studies. The only thing that matters is that you become comfortable with a method of learning that works for you. You can experiment with this during your first semester. Whether it is highlighting, writing out notes or outlines, using flashcards, or discussing contents with fellow students, find out what combination of methods works for you. I have a good visual memory and in medical school I would watch TV while I studied anatomy. I can remember gross anatomy tests where I was able to recall information by visualizing the shows I was watching and was able to answer questions. If you can leave your freshman year having an effective method of studying, then you can put all of your energy into learning in the following years.

As a physician, it is important to have a good understanding of different people and religions. You can use courses in literature, religion and sociology/anthropology to become better informed and well rounded. The more you understand people the better you will be able to recognize their problems and needs. If you don't feel you will do well in these classes, then take them pass-fail or audit them so you can learn the material without affecting your GPA.

Take advantage of the learning opportunities from seeing lectures by visiting professors to your school. This does not have to be limited to your area of interest. I was fortunate to see many great speakers including Maya Angelou and Steven J. Gould. It is a unique experience to see these remarkable people and learn from them.

If there is a uniquely talented teacher at your school, take or audit their class. There are usually one or several really good teachers at any given college/university whose teaching stands out. Exposure to such talent can be a life-changing event.

Don't take a pre-med course or any other course with a professor who has an anti-premed bias. For the pre-med courses try to switch to another teacher or drop the course for that year, if possible. You can't allow your career to be threatened by someone who has a bias against medical school. For example, one of my physics professors made it very clear that he did not support pre-meds and did flat grading of tests to insure that few students got high grades in his class.

It is very important to get a good academic advisor who is knowledgeable of your needs as a pre-med. Your advisor must have a positive attitude towards pre-meds and the needs of pre-med students. When you are assigned your advisor, ask upper level students who have had that advisor if they were knowledgeable and supportive. If your advisor is anti-pre-med or from a field where they don't have much knowledge of what it takes to be a successful pre-med then you need to switch advisors. Talk with upper level pre-meds and find out who the good advisors are. You can't be shy about demanding change. You are a consumer spending a lot of money for college and you should get the advisor who will be most helpful to your career goals. Many students have accepted bad advisors who have given them advice, which has hurt their chances of getting into medical school. Don't accept a bad advisor.

Research

Working on a basic research project is beneficial in many ways. As a college student it gives you the opportunity to gain expertise in a specialized field by doing the necessary reading to understand and contribute to a cutting edge project. Once you are familiar with the basic goals of the project, you can contribute to the team with ideas and dedicated work. Doing research is beneficial because it puts you in a work situation with a range of people from MDs and PhDs, postdoctoral and graduate students, and research technicians. This tiered team is similar to the teams that you will be a part of as a medical student, resident, and eventually as an attending physician. It is also useful to have a basic understanding of research to be able to critically read research papers and understand new developments when you become a practicing doctor.

When looking for a research project, it is very important to find a lab where you are treated well and participate as part of the team. Big labs appear attractive but often treat lower level students badly. Choosing a lab run by a researcher who values college students' contributions and learning is very important. The best way to find out about the labs on campus is to talk with other students who are doing research in those laboratories. If you have developed a good relationship with a faculty member, you may be able to work in their laboratory or get a recommendation from them of another laboratory that would be a good fit. If you live near a major medical center, you can see what papers are being published in your areas of interest and try to speak with people working in those labs. Your faculty member or mentor may have a connection to one of these laboratories and may be able to assist you. Doing research during school is a big time commitment and you want it to pay off. You must do research to make sure you end up in a lab where you can learn, actively participate, and get a good recommendation letter when you finish. If you can't find this situation, you are better off doing something else rather than having a bad experience or getting a bad recommendation.

Doing a research project will also give you the opportunity to present your work at your school and possibly at a local or national meeting. This is an excellent opportunity to work on your communication skills. Being able to explain your work to different groups of people with different educational backgrounds is a good skill to learn. This will help prepare you to be a doctor where you interact with a range of people from patients to nurses and other doctors on a daily basis.

·CHAPTER ELEVEN·

ADVICE FOR INTERNATIONAL STUDENTS

You may have heard from other students, faculty, or administrators that gaining admission to U.S. medical schools as an international student is difficult. Unfortunately unlike other rumors, this one is actually true. According to the AAMC, in 2018-19, 1,195 international students applied[1] and 97 matriculated.[2] Given that the overall admission rate to medical school is around 40%, you may wonder why the admission rate is so much lower for international students. There are a number of factors that contribute to this:

Only about half of U.S. medical schools will even consider international student applicants.

Most public medical schools do not accept applications from international students because part of their mission is to train physicians that will hopefully stay in state. This is why government funding at the state level makes up a portion of public medical schools' operating budget. Private medical schools do not have this same reliance on state funding and are therefore more open to considering international students.

The AAMC's Medical School Admissions Requirements[3] will show you whether a school accepts applications from international students and often the school's website will also have this information.

International students are not eligible for federal student loans.

One of the major ways students pay for medical school is through federal student loans such as the Stafford and Perkins. These loans are only open to U.S. citizens. Many medical schools are concerned international students may not be able to secure the finances needed to cover tuition, living, and other costs. As a result, it is common for medical schools to request that international students demonstrate their ability to pay for the cost of all four years of medical school.

International students may have a hard time getting visas to stay in the U.S. after completing medical school.

During medical school, international students can legally be in the U.S. on a student visa but after graduating, they are no longer eligible for that type of visa. Given that you need to complete a residency program to receive training in your medical specialty and to become licensed as a physician, schools become concerned that international students may not be able to stay in the U.S. and fully complete their training. You are eligible to use Optional Practical

Training (OPT) time to stay in the U.S. but this will not be long enough to complete your residency.

While some academic medical centers will sponsor visas for residents in their program, others will not. Some medical student affairs offices provide information about this, as do Graduate Medical Education offices at specific schools. Residency programs themselves also note whether they sponsor visas or not.[4]

How to Become a Competitive Applicant as an International Student

If you are an international student, you need to make strategic choices beyond just the basics needed to position yourself well for the application cycle. You have a lot to contribute to the field of medicine and taking the following steps can show medical schools that you will be a great addition to their incoming class.

Be able to tell your unique story.

My most successful international students did an outstanding job throughout the application process of sharing their life story and the lessons they learned along the way. You truly bring a unique and special perspective so you need to convey that in every stage of the application process. One student spent part of his personal statement talking about the skills he developed while completing mandatory military service in his home country. Another highlighted the economic disparities she observed within her home city in Africa and how that affected medical care. If you're not sure how to tell your story or what parts of your experiences to highlight, reach out to your pre-med advisor, a trusted mentor, or someone else who knows you well.

Choose a major that will give you the option of gaining research and/or clinical experience here during summers.

As part of the terms of your student visa, you have what is called Curricular Practical Training (CPT). The downside of CPT is that in order to be in the U.S. during the summer and participate in an internship or other opportunity, that activity has to be directly related to your course of study. For example, if you are majoring in Anthropology but want to do clinical research at an academic medical center over the summer, you would not be permitted to do so. A way to address this is to have at least one major in a science-related field or a subject that still has ties to research (psychology, etc.). Some of my advisees picked a science major that aligned closely with the prerequisite courses for medical school and then did another major or minor in a subject of interest such as a language, economics, or other areas. This does not mean you have to double major but it does mean you have to choose your major carefully. Speak with the campus office that works with international students and also discuss this with your pre-med advisor.

Get to know faculty, research mentors, and others well enough that when you request letters of recommendation, the letters will reflect an in-depth connection between you and the letter writer.

I have worked with many international students who had outstanding GPAs, top MCAT scores, and a solid record of clinical, research, and other experiences. The element of their application that was lacking was their letters of recommendation. Many faculty members' letters would be quite short and essentially say, "This student was exceptional" but not much else. There was no evidence of a connection beyond that of what the professor saw in class and on exams.

As an international student, it is important to develop academic and professional relationships where people get to know you on a deeper level. Plan on going to professors' office hours, engaging in research with them, or getting involved in a club with a faculty member advisor. In your activities outside of the classroom, form meaningful relationships with your co-workers, supervisor, peers, or members of the community.

Gain clinical experience in the U.S.

While it is fine to shadow physicians and/or volunteer at a hospital or other healthcare facility in your home country, medical schools want to see that you have an understanding of the U.S. healthcare system. There are a number of ways to gain this experience (as noted in Chapter 9). This is an additional way to expand your communication.

Demonstrate your communication skills both in your written application and during interviews.

This is a sensitive topic but is something you need to be aware of as you move through the application process. As they decide whether to invite you for an interview, medical schools closely examine your written application materials and look at your score in the Critical Analysis and Reasoning Skills (CARS) portion of the MCAT. If they have any concerns about your ability to communicate effectively, they will not move forward with your application. It is essential to make sure your primary and secondary application essays are well written and do not contain any typos or grammatical issues. In terms of the MCAT, if your CARS score is significantly lower than your other three section scores, you should strongly consider retaking the exam.

If you are invited to interview, your ability to communicate verbally will be assessed. Even if your written application is flawless, medical schools need to have confidence that you will be able to speak with patients effectively as well as interact with your colleagues. If English is a relatively new language for you or you struggle in extended conversations, make it a priority to practice speaking with people in a lot of different settings. This is where volunteer work and other activities that get you out into the community can be extremely helpful.

You should also consider scheduling a mock interview with your pre-med advisor or at your college or university's Career Services office. At some schools, your mock interview can be recorded so you can review the playback with your advisor. This also gives you the chance to practice how to answer specific questions.

PART III

THE APPLICATION PROCESS

· CHAPTER TWELVE ·

PREPARING TO APPLY

Consider which application cycle may be best for you (after junior year, senior year, or beyond).

As I noted earlier, far fewer students go directly from their undergraduate studies to medical school than did in the past. In fact, many medical schools report that 60-70% or more of the students in their incoming class have taken a year off before starting medical school. Why? Applying after your senior year gives you more time to become a competitive applicant (more time for MCAT prep, your senior year grades count, etc.). While this time is often referred to as a gap year, I think it is better to look at it as a year of opportunity. Many students have interests they want to pursue before starting their medical education.

There was an amazing student I worked with who had a strong interest in environmental science as well as medicine. He decided that rather than going straight to medical school after graduating, they wanted to delve into environmental research further. He applied to medical school during the year after he graduated from college and while he was completing a research Fulbright Fellowship in the rainforests of South America studying epiphyte plants. He was accepted to multiple medical schools and is thriving. I know he will become an outstanding doctor who is well liked and respected by patients and colleagues. The student knew that he did want to become a doctor but also knew he had other intellectual interests. His choice to do environmental research ended up making him a more competitive applicant for medical school and also meant he entered medical school with a clear focus having given himself the time and space to pursue other passions.

I have had other students who completed service in Peace Corps after graduating and before going to medical school. Another popular choice is to do full-time research positions at the National Institutes of Health or academic medical centers. The medical schools will still be there...give yourself the time and chance to pursue your other goals!

If your academic record isn't strong enough by the end of college, you may need to do a record-enhancer post-baccalaureate program or Special Master's program before applying.

As you begin to review schools you are interested in and you find you are outside of the range for the GPA of accepted students in previous cycles, you will need to strengthen your track record of academic success before applying. Medical schools look at GPA to determine whether they think you can thrive in their curriculum. If you don't have evidence of success especially in science courses, then you have some work to do.

You have two main options. The first is a record-enhancer post-baccalaureate program where you would take advanced undergraduate coursework that would continue to improve your undergraduate science GPA. The second option is to complete a Special Master's program in which you would take graduate level courses. Many Special Master's programs are based at medical schools and if you perform well in the program, it can help you become more competitive at that school. Some medical schools that have partnerships with Master's programs offer a provisional acceptance to the medical school pending a certain academic and MCAT performance.

As you research these options, you need to keep in mind that wherever you decide to go, you have to do extremely well there. Getting a B or B+ average is not going to help you. Look at the program's curriculum, advising support, and other factors and carefully assess where you think you can excel. Also, try to talk to alumni who are either currently in one of those programs or who completed one and are now in medical school. It is likely that they considered other programs before choosing theirs and they can give you insight into how they made their decision as well as what they think of their program.

DECIDING WHERE TO APPLY

Create a target list of schools to apply to where you will be competitive not just in terms of GPA and MCAT scores.

The Medical School Admissions Requirements (MSAR)[1] compiled annually by the AAMC provides detailed information about GPA and MCAT ranges for schools and also includes the schools' mission statements and key facts. A free version provides limited details and the fee-based version provides the full range of information (it's $28 for the 2019 version). I am not an AAMC salesperson; I simply feel it is the most comprehensive and accurate source of information about medical schools.

Creating your school list isn't as cut and dry as simply looking at your numbers and different schools' numbers and deciding where you are competitive. Rather than only obsessing about where you fall in a school's range, spend your time researching the personality of each of your prospective schools and whether they align with your background. Just like pre-meds, medical schools have very different personalities. Some are more research-oriented (for example, Duke) whereas others value students with a strong track record of service (Pritzker) or embrace students who march to the beat of their own drummer (Brown). The more you know about a school's personality, the better positioned you are to decide whether it would be a good fit for you and whether you're the type of student they're looking for.

In addition to doing research on schools' personalities, it's also valuable to ask yourself the following questions:

- Would I be considered an in-state resident? This affects admissions at state medical schools and can also make a huge difference in tuition.

- How many students are in each entering class? This varies a lot - some of the smaller medical schools have less than 90 people per class whereas the largest have up to 250 students per class.

- Do I like the location? You're spending four years there - is it a place where you feel comfortable?

How many schools should you apply to? In 2018-19, the average nationally per applicant was 16 schools.[2] Even applying to that high a number, a lot of students get accepted to 1-3 schools if that. If you get more than 3 acceptances, that's wonderful! I think around the average number is fine but if you feel more comfortable applying to more, that's ok. Just remember that you are going to have to submit secondary applications for the vast majority of those schools (more about secondary applications is below). Remember, think about what schools would be a good fit...not just academically, but overall.

I wanted to address the topic of Early Decision, since many of you may have chosen that option during the college application process. It is risky to apply this way for medical school since you can only submit your AMCAS (primary application) for that one school. They would decide whether or not to interview you and then they must share their admissions decision with you by October 1st. If you do not get in, you can apply to other schools but it is already so late in the cycle that you may end up having to reapply in the next cycle. It also does not give you the same advantage that Early Decision does in college. Since medical schools have thousands of applicants for a small number of places in their incoming class, they don't have an incentive to admit students who may not be as competitive if they were in the general pool. As a result, very few applicants choose this option. If you are thinking about applying Early Decision, discuss this with your pre-med advisor but keep the risks in mind.

Thoroughly research the schools online.

Go beyond just looking at the Admissions pages of their website. If you can, look at the pages for current students or any pages related to student life. Those are going to give you some insight into what life is like there for students. For example, Washington University School of Medicine in St. Louis does an annual student-produced "Dis-Orientation Guide" that really gives you a flavor for life as a WashU medical student.[3] Also, become familiar with the hospital(s) affiliated with the medical school and the types of initiatives going on. If you're interested in alternative medicine, see if they have a complementary and alternative health department or center. If service is your thing, see if they have a free clinic run by residents and medical students. All of these pieces of information will help you learn more about different schools and assess mutual fit.

Work with your pre-professional advising office.

Having an appointment with a pre-professional advisor is also helpful when deciding where to apply. Generally, you should come to your appointment prepared with a preliminary list of schools to discuss. S/he will be able to provide feedback on the list and whether there are schools you may want to add and eliminate.

Talk to people who are either currently attending or graduated from the medical school(s) you are considering.

Your pre-professional advising office and/or your alumnae affairs office at your college/university should be able to help with this.

Most schools have searchable alumni databases where you can view where people went to graduate or professional school. You can also use web resources like LinkedIn to search for people who attended your undergraduate institution and went on to medical school.

Remember who you know and tap into your network! Maybe your doctor knows someone they can put you in touch with. Once you identify the people you want to contact, reach out to them via email or phone. Inquire if they would be willing to have a brief conversation with you to share their perspective on their medical school experience. Get their overall views but also prepare a few questions about topics you're interested in and aspects of the school that are important to you.

GEARING UP FOR THE CYCLE

Plan on submitting your primary application early in the cycle.

The American Medical College Application Service (AMCAS), which is the primary application for medical school, opens in early May for you to begin working on it and you are able to submit beginning in early June. The sooner you submit, the sooner it will enter the queue to be verified. The verification process is where AMCAS staff members compare your official transcript(s) (you must request these from any college/university you have attended) with the courses and grades you have manually entered in the application. They will then compute all of your different GPAS including BCPM (Biology, Chemistry, Physics, and Math), AO (All Other classes), and your Cumulative GPA. This process can take several weeks and many medical schools will not send you a secondary application until they receive your verified primary application.

Medical schools won't review your file to decide on interview invitations until they have 4 pieces of information: your verified AMCAS application, your secondary application, your MCAT score, and your letters of recommendation. The later your file becomes complete, the later your application gets read by medical schools, and the later you will even be considered for interviews. Imagine if you don't submit the AMCAS until September. It won't be verified until late September/early October and you would be writing your secondary essays in mid October. Let's assume your MCAT score and recommendation letters were in at that point so your file became complete in mid October. Many schools are still reading complete files from July and August at that point. So, your file may not be read until December and you might be invited for an interview in January or February. At that point, a significant number of seats in their incoming class have already been filled. Even if you are a solid applicant, if you apply late, you are dramatically increasing the chances that you will not get any acceptances and will end up having to reapply.

Set aside money for the application process.

Between primary and secondary application fees, traveling to interviews, and other costs, the application process can easily exceed several thousand dollars. Plan ahead and start saving for this and budget accordingly.

You should also check to see if you are eligible for the Fee Assistance Program (FAP). If you receive this benefit, you will get MCAT registration at half price, receive free prep materials, and be able to designate 15 schools on AMCAS (your primary application) for free. Often medical schools will waive their secondary application fee for anyone who is an FAP recipient. Every applicant should at least explore whether they are eligible for this. Details about the FAP can be found on the Association of American Medical Colleges' website.[4]

Clean up your social media accounts.

In an article on the application process, the Association of American Medical Colleges quotes Scott M. Rodgers, MD, associate dean for medical student affairs at Vanderbilt University School of Medicine, who shares: "Every student should assume that admissions committees DO look up applicants online and sometimes come across information about people that can either hurt or help a candidate."[5] I heard stories from several admissions deans who said their student interviewers liked to look up the applicants they were going to speak with and then shared information with the admissions committee about what they found. One dean shared that he discovered that an applicant had a picture of himself on Facebook doing a keg stand and engaging in other questionable behavior. This led to the applicant being denied admission. For any of your social media accounts, carefully review your privacy settings and consider taking down any images or comments that might cause a medical school to be concerned about your professionalism and judgment.

Avoid application season burnout.

This is a very long, emotionally draining process so it is vital to keep yourself healthy and reduce your stress. Having a creative outlet is very important and actually makes you a more interesting and stronger applicant. Taking time every day or every few days to sketch, compose music, write a short story, choreograph a dance routine, or do something completely different from the Organic Chemistry or Physics you're studying will help you feel renewed and energized.

Numerous studies over the years have demonstrated the physical and emotional benefits of being active. This doesn't mean you have to go to the gym and run on the treadmill every day. The key is to find an activity you enjoy that also gets your heart rate up. It might be karate or salsa dancing or rock climbing or quidditch (for you Harry Potter fans out there!). Staying fit will also help you be better able to handle stress.

Finding a few minutes to focus on your breathing and clear your mind is a great way to avoid burnout. Some students gravitate towards more formal meditation, which is fine. There are a lot of guided meditations that you can download from iTunes or other sources if you feel this type of meditation works best for you. I also highly recommend reading Leo Babauta's blog called Zen Habits[6] or any other blogs that help you reflect and relax. No matter how you choose to do so, make sure you have a few minutes a day of just being a person instead of being in pre-med mode 24-7.

Put a strong support network in place.

You need people in your life who are in your corner throughout this process. It's good to have people who are cheerleaders, who keep you accountable for meeting deadlines, and make you laugh. Sometimes it's a few people who fulfill multiple roles or you may have friends/family members who each fulfill one of these roles. Maybe one friend is in charge of sending you links to cat videos or memes that make you laugh. Another option is to schedule a weekly coffee chat or phone call with a person so that you can tell them everything you did for the application process that week. Your family and friends care about you and are often delighted if you give them a job to do so that they can help you during the application process.

Create a tracking system for yourself.

There are a lot of deadlines and details to keep track of in the application process. It is a good idea to build a tracking system so that you are on top of everything. You can use a spreadsheet or Google document or if you prefer writing it all down and having a binder or folder system to store your notes, that's fine too. The best tracking system is the one you actually use!

· CHAPTER THIRTEEN ·

THE MCAT

Embrace the fact that as a physician, you will be taking timed multiple choice tests your whole career.

Many applicants assume that the MCAT score is just like the SAT and is only a hurdle to clear in the medical school admissions process. Since test taking has become a professional skill needed throughout a physician's entire career, the MCAT is more significant. All of the 3 Steps of the United States Medical Licensing Exam (USMLE) as well as Board certification and recertification are day-long timed multiple-choice tests. Low MCAT scores cause concern because they can indicate a weakness in an applicant's ability to handle timed multiple-choice exams and may raise questions about whether they will be able to pass board exams.

For those of you who are picturing yourselves as surgeons, dermatologists, or any other highly competitive specialty, it is even more important for you to become a very strong test taker. Residency programs place a lot of emphasis on your USMLE Step 1 score (the exam you take at the end of your second year of medical school). A low score can virtually eliminate you from consideration.

This means that if you have always said, "I'm not good at standardized tests," you need to banish that thought from your mind. Your performance on these types of tests can improve with time and practice. You need to make developing this skill a priority.

If you experience test-taking anxiety, you need to address it now rather than waiting until you take the MCAT.

The worst thing to do is know you have major test taking anxiety, do nothing about it, and then have those feelings undermine your success on the MCAT. Seek assistance from your campus office of Disability Services and/or your doctor to see what options you have for addressing your test taking anxiety. Meditation and other stress relief techniques can also be helpful. The bottom line is that you need to do whatever you can to position yourself for success.

If you have any physical or mental conditions for which you get accommodations at your school, consider applying for accommodations on the MCAT.

One of my advisees had severe Crohn's disease and needed extended break times. Another had a learning difference that meant she receive extended time on exams. Both were able to apply for and receive accommodations on the MCAT exam and both successfully gained admission to medical school.

A lot of applicants who have a condition for which they may receive accommodations don't even apply for them because they think medical schools will see that they were granted these accommodations. Your score report looks identical to someone who did not receive extended time or any other accommodation. You owe it to yourself to explore whether you might be able to receive accommodations.

The Association of American Medical Colleges requires documentation and other information in order for you to apply. Their website provides step-by-step guidance on the process of applying for accommodations. You should also work with your campus office of Disability or Accessibility Services, especially if you received accommodations during college.

Create an effective study plan that includes taking a lot of practice tests.

Much like studying for science courses, some students I have met with were studying for the MCAT by simply rereading their notes from science classes and reading chapters of MCAT prep books. I strongly recommended doing a lot of practice tests and using other active methods to retain the subject knowledge needed. In one case, a student who used the new study methods we discussed together increased his score by 10 points.

Just reading MCAT prep books or your notes is not enough. You need to spend a significant amount of time doing practice problems, test sections, and full-length tests. The new MCAT, which debuted in April 2015, is now over seven and a half hours long and includes four sections:[1]

- Biological and Biochemical Foundations of Living Systems

- Chemical and Physical Foundations of Biological Systems

- Psychological, Social, and Biological Foundations of Behavior

- Critical Analysis and Reasoning Skills

You need to train for it as an endurance event. Also, if your college or university did not administer many timed multiple-choice tests, you need to spend time practicing and getting comfortable with this format. It is very different from a short answer or essay-based exam. Being able to manage your time effectively within sections is very important.

The AAMC has an excellent tool called "What's on the MCAT Exam?"[2] and I specifically like the PDF you can download, which contains an outline of all of the topics that can be tested. You can use this outline as a way to double-check your content knowledge and see what you need to focus more time on. For example, you might highlight the outline using green as "I know this", yellow as "I kind of know this but am not really sure", and red or pink as "I don't know this or don't remember it." You can then build your content review around this, allocating more time for the areas you are not as solid in rather than spending equal amounts of time on what you know and don't know.

Assess whether a prep class or tutoring might be right for you.

If I had a dollar for every pre-med who asked me whether they had to take an MCAT prep class, I would be on a beach somewhere right now! There are a lot of factors to consider as you decide whether a prep class is worth it for you. Are you good at sticking to time you have set aside for studying or do you need the accountability of being in a class? Did you take an SAT prep class in high school and if so, was it helpful? Also, it is good to speak with seniors and alumni from your school about whether or not they took a class and whether they thought it was helpful. Plus, your school may offer some MCAT prep or potentially provide space for a test prep company to teach a class on campus.

Do not wait until the last minute to start studying.

One very talented student who had a great GPA and strong experiences ended up with an MCAT that was lower than where I thought he would score. He admitted that he started studying about 3 weeks before the exam and took his first and only practice test a few days before taking the actual exam. The score reflected the fact that he didn't devote enough time to prepare for the exam.

Give yourself ample time to study. I think at least 3-4 months is the minimum you would want to devote to MCAT prep. Again, you need to give yourself time for content review as well as a lot of practice tests.

Take the MCAT early in the application cycle.

I met with a student who was planning to take the MCAT in late August and then applying. I advised him that was very late and it would most likely have a negative impact on his application. He went forward anyway and did not gain admission to medical school that cycle.

You need to take the MCAT relatively early in the cycle in which you are applying or even before that. For example, if you are applying during the summer after junior year, you would want to take the MCAT no later than one of the June dates. There is a domino effect that happens when you take the test late. Medical schools will not review your application until your test scores are in. Since it takes a month for test scores to come back, this means you will not have a complete application file at medical schools until mid-fall. They will likely have thousands of applications to read before they even get to yours and by the time they do, a number of spots in their incoming class may already be filled.

If you get a low score, you need to retake the MCAT.

This sounds obvious but you would be surprised how many applicants don't want to retake the MCAT even when they know their score isn't competitive. I was meeting with a reapplicant and in reviewing his application from the previous year, it was clear that his low MCAT score had hurt him. As we discussed his action plan and next steps, I strongly encouraged him to retake the exam. He chose not to and did not get into medical school that second cycle.

If you have a low score in one specific section, you may also have to retake the exam. You don't want any section to be way out of step with the others. A consistent performance across the sections is what you need to aim for and achieve. To see the MCAT average and ranges for schools you are interested in, consult the AAMC's Medical School Admissions Requirements. The medical schools' websites often also include information on their previous incoming class. Additionally, you can speak with your pre-med advisor to learn about the MCAT scores of successful alumni from your specific school.

If you have a low section or overall test score, you need to face the reality that you have to retake it and score better on it. Simply hoping a low score will be offset by great activities will not get you the results you are looking for. You need to diagnose why you did not do well on the first exam and then take tangible steps to prepare in a better way and increase your score.

CHAPTER FOURTEEN

COMPLETING THE AMCAS APPLICATION

Create your application account right when the cycle opens.

Getting your account up and running as early as possible is a good idea. You can then work on sections when you are ready rather than just doing everything at once. The sections that are good to complete right away are the Biographical and the Schools Attended areas.

Have the AMCAS application manual PDF open in a browser tab at all times you are working on the application.

The AMCAS application manual is your go-to resource for every section of the application. It is usually well over 100 pages and every page is packed with key details you need to read carefully and know. I highly recommend reading through it and then keeping it open so you can refer to it throughout the process.

Have an official transcript sent to you a few weeks before you have transcripts sent to AMCAS and start the Course-

work portion of AMCAS. Double-check it to ensure it is error-free and then use it to manually type in your courses in AMCAS.

Getting your transcript before you have your Registrar's office send it to AMCAS is important since sometimes there may be errors on it. For example, one applicant noticed that all of their prerequisite courses except for one listed that the courses were lecture & lab so they were able to get the Registrar to update the title that was missing that information. Other students noticed that their AP coursework was listed incorrectly. Go over your official transcript carefully to make sure everything is listed as it should be.

Since the AMCAS staff uses the official transcripts they get from your school(s) when they complete the verification process, you want to make sure you are entering your courses in AMCAS as they appear on that document. Enter the course numbers, titles, grades, and other details as they are listed in the official transcript. This can save you a lot of potential issues and having your application returned to you by AMCAS.

Request official transcripts from anywhere you took college coursework and have them sent to AMCAS.

One applicant mistakenly thought that his college would automatically send AMCAS his official transcript. Luckily, I was able to catch this misunderstanding on the student's part and let the student know that he needed to submit a request to the Registrar's office to have the transcript sent. Once you complete the Schools Attended section, you can generate Transcript Request forms. Send the form to the Registrar's office of each college you attended. You can do this well before you submit your AMCAS application and I encourage you to do so. If you wait until after you submit your AMCAS, then your application will just be in limbo until your transcripts arrive. They can't start the verification process until they have all of your transcripts. Even if you transferred courses from other schools to your main college/university, you often still need to get an official transcript sent from those other schools. Check the AMCAS manual about your specific situation.

Remember that the AMCAS will be transmitted to all of the medical schools you designate.

The AMCAS is not the place to put any school-specific details, especially in your personal statement or the Work/Activities section. Make sure that everything you write on the AMCAS is information you are fine with all of the schools you apply to being able to see this content. Secondary applications are when you get to answer school-specific essay questions.

Be strategic about what you include in the Work/Activities section and which ones you select as your most meaningful activities.

On the AMCAS application, you have 15 spaces in which to list all of your different experiences and activities. Often applicants have done far more than 15 noteworthy items. If you are pressed for space, you can group similar experiences into one entry. For example, if you have received multiple academic awards, you can put those together and just choose a date range that encompasses when you received them. Also, you do not have to list every activity, club, and experience you have ever done. For example, if you were on the club soccer team for one semester during your freshman year, you may want to leave that off in favor of putting something more significant from another time in your college career.

In the description portion of each entry, a good approach to take is to address what the experience was, what your role was in it, and what you learned from it. While you don't get much space, you should be able to cover each of these items. This enables the reader to picture what you did and why it mattered.

You also get to designate three of the fifteen as most meaningful activities. This gives you an additional 1,325 characters to describe these activities in more depth. These do not all have to be medically related activities. Choose experiences that really shaped you as a person and talk about why they had a significant impact on you.

If you have had to work during college, definitely include this in the Work/Activities section.

While related to the tip above, this is specifically for those of you who worked on and/or off campus. You may not think your cashier job at Target is something medical schools would want to know but they do want to hear about it for several reasons. First, if you worked while also going to school, it is helpful for you to account for the time you spent on the job. Also, customer service jobs often involve working with people from diverse backgrounds as well as solving problems. These are skills that can be useful in medicine.

CHAPTER FIFTEEN

PERSONAL STATEMENT *&* SECONDARY APPLICATIONS

PERSONAL STATEMENT

Make sure to answer the question of why you want to go to medical school.

As part of the American Medical College Application Service (AMCAS), you will have to write a personal statement. You have 5300 characters (including spaces) to address why you want to go to medical school. AACOMAS (the osteopathic application) has even fewer characters. Given the short amount of space available, you need to pick a few of your experiences and highlight why you want to become a doctor. Some applicants get so freaked out that they write about everything and anything but they do not actually answer the question of why they want to go to medical school. You need to make sure you keep that question at the forefront of your mind as you write and edit your personal statement.

Consider incorporating anecdotes.

Essentially, these are mini-stories that enable the reader to gain a stronger sense of your motivation for becoming a physician. Rather than being general (for example, "I enjoyed volunteering at a retirement home"), you can talk about a specific person or event that shaped you. If you do talk about a specific patient, use a different name for them.

Have a core theme.

It is great to have a central message you are trying to convey and then make sure that the different experiences you weave into the essay connect back with that point. Since medical schools have read about all of your experiences in the Work/Activities section, you only need to pick a few key experiences to write about in your personal statement rather than doing a narrative version of your resume. For example, maybe your theme is teaching and learning. You could start the essay with an anecdote about observing a physician explaining a diagnosis to her patients and how you were inspired by her ability to convey the information in a way that her patients could receive and process it instead of finding it confusing. You could then transition into your own teaching experiences, whether you mentored or tutored younger kids or served as a teaching assistant in college. Finally, you could close by discussing learning and how critical a commitment to lifelong learning is, especially as a physician. Other core themes could be the body in motion, the impact of loss, public health, global health challenges, resilience, etc.

You do not have to be linear.

I have seen a lot of personal statements that started out when the writer was a child. From what deans have shared with me, this is not a great approach because they begin to picture little you, not the grown-up you who will become a great doctor. If you have a profound childhood experience that motivated you to become a physician, you do not have to have it as the beginning of your essay. Here is one technique that I have seen applicants use very successfully:

1. Start with a recent anecdote that has a connection to the childhood experience they want to share. For example, "While shadowing a pediatrician, I often got to observe her treating children diagnosed with diabetes. As I watched an eight-year old girl struggle to come to terms with complications caused by her diabetes, I felt myself remembering my little sister Grace's own battles with the disease."

2. Have the middle section of your essay be on the childhood experience. For example, "After the night my sister went into diabetic shock, I couldn't learn enough about the disease. I spoke with her doctors and nurses and read every article I could. This early interest grew into a passion for the diabetes research that I pursued during college."

3. Close the essay in the present. For example, "I will always re-member Grace's experiences but by observing and speaking with numerous diabetic patients, I gained a broader perspective. Witnessing and exploring the impact that diabetes has

on patients has made me even more passionate about joining the fight against this disease. In medical school, I hope to expand my clinical and research skills so that I can provide outstanding care to my patients while also gaining new insights into the disease and ways to treat it."

Don't use quotes or name drop.

How many times do you think admissions deans have read, "Be the change you want to see in the world" or quotes along those lines? As amazing as Gandhi was, you should use your own words and experiences rather than relying on the words of others. As for name-dropping, I have seen this really undermine an otherwise fairly good essay. For example, "During my time shadowing Dr. Jones, world-renown Chief of Surgery at Lakeview Hospital..." Focus more on how experiences impacted you instead of emphasizing who they were with. Often, the reason applicants name drop is because they think it may help them at their top choice school. If you feel this way, it is much more appropriate to get a strong recommendation letter from Dr. Jones than to go on and on about her in your essay. Your other option is if you are applying to the same medical school where Dr. Smith trained, you can incorporate your experiences with her into an essay on your secondary application since those are individual to each school.

Do not spend your whole personal statement describing in graphic detail an illness you or a relative experienced.

This may seem like an odd one but what I mean by this is that if you choose to write about your own experience with a serious illness or the experience of a family member or close friend, you need to approach it in a specific way. You don't want to spend a lot of time describing the condition/disease. You also want to make sure that whatever the situation was, you focus on how that illness impacted you. Did seeing your mother's struggle with breast cancer prompt you to take action, whether it was volunteering, doing research, etc.? Did having leukemia as a child inspire you to help children facing the same condition? Keep the focus on you and on answering the "why medical school" question.

Be careful about including any details or experiences that are still emotionally raw for you.

One dean told me about a time when he was interviewing an applicant who had written her personal statement about her mother's battle with cancer. When he asked the applicant about it, the applicant burst into tears. On the one hand, the dean felt sad for this applicant who was clearly very upset but he also felt like if it was a topic that was so tough to talk about, then the applicant should not have included it in her personal statement. If you can discuss a situation in a calm and collected way, then you can probably include it in your personal statement but if it's difficult not to get emotional when talking about that event, then consider leaving it out of your essay.

Use straightforward language, not flowery or overly complicated vocabulary.

"It was a dark and stormy night and my drenched rain coat stuck to my body as I slowly made my way to the brightly illuminated hospital to begin my arduous shift as a volunteer."

Number one, this wastes valuable character space and number two, who speaks like this? This is not the time to write a dramatic short story or think you are being impressive by throwing in every long or complicated word you know.

Do not have a personal statement that uses odd creative writing (for example, writing from the point of view of a stethoscope).

Just don't do this. Admissions committees may think you are missing your calling as a creative writer rather than a future doctor.

Avoid including anything that would make a medical school question your judgment/behavior.

One student sent me a draft of his personal statement that started out by describing how he had gotten up to go for a run on a Sunday morning, even though he was hung over, so he could train for an important race. He thought it demonstrated resilience but I explained to him that medical schools would think it demonstrated poor judgment. Luckily, we worked together to revise his draft and he ended up with a great personal statement that was more about how different people inspired him and why he wanted to become a doctor.

Show, don't tell.

Instead of saying, "I am a compassionate person who is comfortable communicating with others", give examples of experiences that show you embody those qualities. This is where anecdotes can be helpful. When you just list your good qualities without backing them up with evidence, they just feel hollow.

Proofread!

Once you submit your application, you will not be able to edit your personal statement. That's why it is critical that you proofread your statement thoroughly and fix any typos. Spellcheck doesn't pick up when you misuse a word or slightly misspell it and it ends up being another word that is spelled correctly. Here are five cringe-worthy examples of when applicants did not proofread carefully:

> *"I want to peruse a career in medicine."*

> It is medicine, not a magazine! They meant to say: "pursue."

> *"In the future, I plan to sue the lessons I learned during my research experience."*

> They meant to say: "use." Now it sounds like they are headed for a legal battle!

"I want to protest the ability for underserved patients to gain better access to healthcare."

Yikes! They meant to write: "protect" and it is scary how just a one-letter difference made the tone of this sentence shift from noble to discriminatory.

"I was humbled that the patient felt comfortable enough to confine in me."

Clearly, the applicant meant to write: "confide" but again, you can see how one little letter completely changes how this sounds.

"I feel it?s very important to earn a patient?s trust."

In this case, the applicant copied and pasted from a version of Word and it replaced apostrophes with question marks. Saving your essay as plain text or even manually retyping it into the textbox on the application can help you avoid this type of issue.

If your college or university's pre-professional advising office reviews personal statements, have them give you feedback. Otherwise, you can take your essay to the writing center at your school. Some of these services are available after you graduate but if not, have a family member or friend help you catch the typos in your essay.

Pick only a few people (at most) to edit your personal statement and give you feedback.

I was working with one applicant and we had already been through several drafts. Each time, the draft sounded completely different. When I asked the applicant what was going on, she confessed that they had sent it to both of their parents, several professors, and several family friends who are doctors and that every one of those people had different opinions on what the personal statement should say. The applicant was thoroughly confused. After we chatted, we established what was most important for her and she was able to tune out all of those other voices to create a personal statement that really captured her voice and perspective.

After you have added it into the AMCAS application text box, proofread it again!

Since it can sometimes be hard to proofread while looking at your text on a screen, print out a PDF of your AMCAS (the button to generate this is on the AMCAS home page) and then mark it up with a pen so that you catch and correct any typos. You want your reader to focus on the message you are conveying rather than being distracted by errors. Some medical school admissions staff will stop reading an application if they see a lot of typos. Their logic is that if you can't make sure your essay is error-free, you lack attention to important details and might make similar errors in patients' records.

SECONDARY APPLICATION ESSAYS

Know the difference between the personal statement and secondary applications.

The critical difference between the two types of essays is that in the personal statement you are answering the question, "Why medical school in general?" and in your secondary essays, you are answering the question, "Why that specific medical school?" This is a huge difference and is something that often trips up applicants. If you write your secondary essays with more of a general focus on medical school, you have missed a valuable opportunity to separate yourself from the rest of the applicants in a positive way.

Do not copy and paste/recycle answers on multiple secondary applications.

Deans can tell when you are writing the same generic answer plus, if you are not careful, you can make the unforgivable mistake of writing "I am interested in School X" when you meant to say School Y. This happened to one applicant and she asked whether she should contact the school where she had submitted the secondary with the wrong name. At that point, you can't fix that mistake.

Thoroughly research each school and have your secondary essays reflect the knowledge you gain about them.

The best secondary application answers are uniquely customized for that specific school and should show that you have researched their program and identified points of connection. For example, if you volunteered at a homeless clinic and you know that school has one that medical students staff, you can touch on that. Or perhaps they have a lupus research center and that is a disease you are interested in studying. Giving very targeted answers about "Why their school?" is a great way to shine during this step of the application process.

Consider your audience.

Since each school designs the questions on secondary applications, the admissions committee members who read your answers do so in a more in-depth way. They are looking to see whether you have really thought through why their school is a good fit for you and why you are a good fit for them. This is your last chance on paper to show that you are worthy of an interview...make the most of it!

Complete secondary applications in a timely fashion.

Two different applicants in the past few years who I think would have gained admission to medical schools made the mistake of waiting several months to submit their secondary applications. As a result, both have to reapply. You need to turn your secondary applications around and submit them within about 2 weeks. Remember that medical schools won't read your application until you have this in.

· CHAPTER SIXTEEN ·

INTERVIEWING

Know the timeline for the interview season.

The medical school interview season begins in late August and while some schools began sending out acceptances in mid-October, many medical schools interview candidates well into mid-February and in a few cases, even into March and April.

Take CASPer if required by specific medical schools.

Some medical schools are starting to require applicants to take CASPer, which is a situational judgment test administered online. It consists of 12 video or written scenarios with three questions each and it is supposed to assess skills including communication, collaboration, equity, professionalism, problem solving, empathy, motivation, and ethics.[1] If a medical school requires this test, it will be specified either within their application portal where you submit your secondary applications and track your application or you may be notified another way.

Understand the questions your interviewer is thinking about as s/he speaks with you.

Here are a few of the questions interviewers often have in mind while they are speaking with you:

- Is this applicant as good or better in person than s/he is on paper?

- Would I trust this applicant to treat a member of my family?

- Would I want this applicant as a colleague? (Or, put another way, would I want to go on a long car ride with this person or be stuck in an airport with him/her if our flight got cancelled?)

Understanding what they are looking for is extremely critical both during your preparation and during the interview itself.

Do in-depth research on each school where you are invited to interview.

Skimming the admissions website for the school where you are interviewing is not enough. You need to think about mutual fit (why you are a good fit for them and they are a good fit for you), what makes them stand out, and why you want to become a physician. Preparing for interviews is another time when you can draw on your research into schools. You need to be able to answer both the "Why medical school" and the "Why our medical school?" questions. Steer clear of the "You're so prestigious" answers...schools have heard these a million times. A personalized answer that reflects your knowledge of the school is always the best. For example, "I'm drawn to your medical school for several reasons. First, in speaking with alumni, they consistently mentioned the strong mentoring relationship between faculty and students. I am excited about forming this type of relationship here and know it will enhance my learning experience. Second, your emphasis on collaborative care and interacting with allied health professionals really appeals to me. I noticed that you have a center for integrated learning that is open to physicians, nurses, physical therapists, and that medical students get to attend training sessions there. Finally, I feel this is the best place for me to grow as a future clinician. One of the alums I spoke with specifically mentioned how he felt the clinical foundation he received here helps him every day in his conversations with patients. Having seen his skills in action while spending time with him in his clinic, I want to emulate his warm, open communication style and the rapport he was able to build with his patients. Coming here will help me gain the skills I need to thrive in working with patients."

As you are researching each school where you will be interviewing, creating a document where you track similar information will be helpful. This would include things such as key data related to the school (enrollment, etc.), unique features (maybe they have a center for integrative medicine), and your main motivating factors for wanting to go there. This is helpful to read through in the days and hours leading up to your interview.

Re-read all of your application materials (AMCAS and the secondary application you completed for that school).

Many medical schools do what is called an open file interview. This means they have access to everything that you have submitted as well as your letters of recommendation. Often, interviewers will ask questions about specific experiences you many have written about in your Work/Activities section, your personal statement, and/or your secondary application. Be ready to talk about anything you have written.

Learn about and prepare for the different interview types medical schools use.

Each medical school has complete freedom in determining the length and format of their interviews. Some have it be a half or full day experience that includes interviews, a tour of the school, lunch with medical students, and Q&A sessions. Others have a more condensed process. It's helpful to understand the common types of interview formats and prepare accordingly.

The most common type of interview is still the one-on-one conversation. Lasting anywhere from 30 minutes to an hour, you will speak with a person (a physician and/or faculty member, a medical student, etc.) about your experiences. These interviews can either be open file, meaning that the interviewer is able to read all of the details in your application (AMCAS, recommendation letters, etc.) or closed file, where the interviewer may only know your name and very little else. In these interviews, the goal is to form a good connection with the person and be able to articulate who you are, what you have done, and why you are a good fit for that medical school.

An emerging format that continues to increase in popularity is the Multiple Mini Interview. Originally implemented in Canadian medical schools, MMIs have now expanded to U.S. medical schools. The MMI format involves 8-10 stations where you are given a short prompt to read and about 3 minutes to think about your answer. You then spend about 6-8 minutes with an interviewer discussing your answer. Once completed, you move on to the next station.

Think about possible answers to common questions.

You will almost always be asked a question such as, "Tell me about yourself" at the beginning of the interview. It is good to practice an answer to this question since it is easy to go on tangents and speak for too long. Medical schools often ask, "Why our medical school?" and/or "Why do you want to become a doctor?" It is important to think about these questions in advance and have strong answers for them. You are virtually guaranteed these will come up so it's best to be ready.

Research issues related to medical ethics and reflect on how you might handle specific scenarios.

Medical schools have started posing ethical questions on a number of topics and scenarios. With these questions, it is as much about seeing how you think and react as how you actually answer. They want to see your problem-solving skills and ability to handle different situations.

For example, you may be asked a question such as, "What would you do if you saw one of your classmates struggling with substance abuse in medical school?" When answering, you would want to articulate specific steps you might take. For example, "First, I would try to have a conversation with my classmate and see if there were any ways I could assist them. I would also share any resources I think might be helpful, such as reminding them about counseling services. If the person continued to struggle, I would determine whether to have a discussion with their advisor or a member of the Student Affairs staff. The most important thing would be to make sure my classmate received the help and support they needed."

Other medical ethics questions may touch on legal matters. For example, you may be asked about your position on medically assisted suicide or abortion. In answering these types of questions, you can always say that you would follow the national and state laws pertaining to that issue and also move forward in a way that would be consistent with the policies of the hospital/clinic where you are treating patients. Let's say you were asked a question about whether it is right to use medical marijuana to treat a child with persistent seizures. You could talk about the fact that if you are in a state where use of medical marijuana is legal, then this might be a treatment option you could discuss with the patient's parents.

Prepare questions to ask your interviewers.

While you do want to make a good impression, you also need to treat your interviews as an additional chance to learn more about the schools. Picture yourself sitting there with 3 acceptances, all to schools you like. What information would you need to help you choose where to go? You definitely want to prepare at least 2-3 questions to ask your interviewers.

Wear appropriate and professional but also comfortable clothing/shoes.

Generally, applicants wear a suit for their interview and keep all other elements of their outfit on the professional side. Be careful about bold accessories and colors. You want to stand out in a good way rather than being memorable for wearing something that was not interview appropriate.

You want to feel as confident as possible rather than feeling that your interview suit is wearing you. If you are getting a new suit, make sure to wear it a few times before your interview day so that you are comfortable in it. If your school offers mock interviews, you may want to wear the exact outfit you plan on wearing to your actual interviews.

Most likely, you will be touring the school and potentially climbing stairs so go with shoes you'll feel good in all day. For women, I highly recommend a chic pair of flats rather than heels. Like your suit, definitely wear these shoes a few times before interview day. Whatever shoes you end up wearing, wear appropriate socks. This may seem like a small and silly detail but a Dean told me a story about an applicant who came to an interview and was otherwise dressed professionally except for the white athletic socks they were wearing!

Be respectful and friendly to everyone you meet.

It always amazed me when I would hear from numerous deans of admissions about applicants who treated the admissions office staff poorly or were unprofessional during their interviews with current medical students. One Dean shared a story where an applicant had interviewed well all day but did not end up getting accepted because he screamed at the administrative support staff when they said they couldn't validate his parking. This can be the kiss of death, even if you think you have aced your other interviews. Treat everyone kindly and professionally.

Keep in mind that student interviewers can often be the harshest critics.

Having sat in on several admissions committee meetings at medical schools, I consistently saw that student interviewers often rated applicants lower than faculty interviewers did. They have great pride that they are attending that school and really want to see evidence that you want to go to that particular medical school rather than medical school in general. Have details ready that show you have done your homework and you know why you want to go to their school. Also, do not be too informal with student interviewers. For example, don't use profanity or be too casual when you speak with them. Treat your interactions with them with the same level of professionalism as you would a faculty interviewer.

Breathe.

It sounds simple but you may be nervous and forget to do this. Just breathe...you'll be fine!

After the interview, write or email thank you notes to your interviewers.

This shows that you respect their time and also gives you an additional opportunity to express your interest in their school.

Capture your thoughts about the interview day while it is still fresh in your mind.

It is helpful to create a document that you can fill out immediately after your interview day. What did you like about the school? What surprised you in a good way or in a negative way? If you had an acceptance letter from that school arrive tomorrow, what would you do? Creating a short summary of your interview day is a great way to reflect on your experiences at a medical school. Given that the time between when you interview and when you may be accepted could be several months, being able to read these summaries can really help if you are deciding between two or more great options.

Be patient about hearing back from schools.

Depending on the medical school, some admissions committees meet every other week and discuss applicants. Most medical schools send acceptances from mid-October through late February whereas others choose to notify all applicants of their admissions status at the same time in the spring. Make sure to read and understand the AAMC Application and Acceptance Protocols for Applicants.[2] These important rules provide you with important information about topics such as whether you can hold multiple acceptances, etc. It may take several weeks to find out your admissions status after an interview or even several months if it's a school that issues all decisions in one big batch.

CHAPTER SEVENTEEN

ACCEPTANCES, WAITLISTS, & REJECTIONS

If you get an acceptance, be excited!

You are going to medical school! You now know you have a seat in a medical school class and you have achieved the first step towards becoming a doctor. Remember that every year, over 30,000 applicants do not get even one acceptance. Even if you only end up with one acceptance, you should be extremely proud and happy.

If you have more than one acceptance, carefully assess where to go.

Beginning with the 2019 application cycle, changes have been made to the process relating to acceptances. Your rights and responsibilities are spelled out in the Application and Acceptance Protocols for Applicants from the Association of American Medical Colleges.[1] On or before April 15th, you have to streamline your acceptances down to no more than three schools and then on April 30th, you must choose the one school you will be attending.

Since you are interviewing over a period of many months, you may receive acceptances throughout that time. You do not need to make an immediate decision. Many medical schools ask you to put down a deposit to hold your spot but it is refundable as long as you withdraw your application from them prior to the dates outlined above.

Take your time, review your notes from interviews, consider contacting students/alumni from that school if you have not already done so, and do a thorough pros and cons review. Also, most schools offer a second look weekend or event, which are definitely worth attending. After you decide, take time to celebrate! You're another step closer to becoming a physician!

If you are waitlisted, continue to demonstrate your interest in the school.

If you receive word from a medical school that you have been waitlisted, send a follow-up email to express your strong continuing interest in the school. You can then send an update email/letter in early April so that it is in your file when the waitlist movement starts. Be careful not to send too many updates. Bombarding the admissions office with constant emails listing every little new thing you have done is not going to help your case. Also, if admissions offices specifically say they do not accept updates, then act in accordance with their policy. This is another example of where quality over quantity in the application process is the right approach.

Many applicants ask about whether they should send a letter of intent where they basically say to a medical school, "If you take me, I will definitely come to your school." These aren't necessarily effective because medical schools may think you are sending a similar letter/email to the other schools. However, a strong letter where you express your continued interest, your recent experiences, and why you are a good fit for their school is helpful.

If you have been accepted to more than one school, consider weighing the financial aid packages from each school.

Being able to compare the financial aid packages different medical schools are offering you and seeing which school(s) offer you scholarship money is an advantage. It allows you to make a much more informed decision about your future and how much your education will end up costing. If you get multiple acceptances, it is fine to put down your deposit to hold a seat and then wait until April to make your final decision. Many medical schools don't send out their aid package information until the back end of the cycle because at that point, they know who they have accepted and can allocate potential scholarships accordingly. Note that some medical schools only give need-based aid, not merit-based scholarships. This is something that each school's financial aid website should state.

If you don't get into medical school during the first cycle you apply, you need to take a hard look at weaknesses in your application or other actions that may have undermined your success.

There are many factors that can contribute to an applicant not getting into medical school. Having a low GPA and/or MCAT is certainly one of them but by no means the only reason. You may not have had sufficient experiences, you may have interviewed poorly (if you got to that stage), you may have applied to schools that were all a reach for you, you may have applied late...the list goes on.

Speak with your pre-med advisor and get their assessment of what may have contributed to this outcome. Also, some medical schools do provide feedback to unsuccessful applicants but generally will not do so until the end of the cycle. It can be hard not to get defensive but it is critical to learn how to improve your candidacy for when you reapply in the future.

You may need to take a cycle off before reapplying.

Depending on what the weaknesses were in your application that led to you not getting accepted, you may need additional time to address them. While it is tempting to reapply right away, if you do so having not fixed the problems, then history will repeat itself. Medical schools do look at whether reapplicants have any new experiences or have addressed weaknesses. If you are serious about wanting to get into medical school, you need to take the steps to make your application stronger before you reapply.

PART IV

YOUR NEXT STEPS

CHAPTER EIGHTEEN

HOW TO PAY FOR MEDICAL SCHOOL

One of the most frequently asked questions I receive from students and parents is how to pay for medical school. According to the AAMC Graduation Questionnaire and Tuition and Student Fees Survey, in 2016, the median cost to attend medical school was $249,000 and the median education debt was $190,000.[1] Given that undergraduates in the Class of 2017 had an average student loan debt of $39,400,[2] many medical students will graduate with debt similar to the median home value in the United States ($226,700 as of April 24, 2019).[3] While there are different options for paying for medical school, it is important to understand that you will likely emerge with debt and you need to be ok with the fact you will be paying off loans for a while.

Scholarship Options

Scholarships for medical school exist on multiple levels. At the federal level, there are several departments that offer scholarships. Each medical school also has their own policy on scholarships including whether or not they offer merit-based aid and any individual scholarships. Additionally, a number of different organizations offer scholarships and grants. Here is an overview of these categories:

Programs through the Federal Government

It is important to note that since these are government-funded programs, only U.S. citizens can apply. As of April 2019, these programs exist in the form outlined below but federal agency budgets and programs are always subject to change.

1. Health Professions Scholarship Program (U.S. Department of Defense)

The U.S. Department of Defense's Medicine + the Military website explains the program: "The HPSP covers civilian medical school tuition, pays for fees, provides a monthly living stipend and includes a signing bonus under certain conditions. This scholarship is offered by the Army, Navy, and Air Force, and the benefits are the same across all three Services."[4] You will owe time serving as a physician in the military after completing your residency training (generally, a year of active duty service for every year of medical school that the military paid for). I am intentionally providing broad brushstrokes rather than fine details here because the best course of action if you are considering this program is to speak with a local recruiter. He/she will be able to give you the most up to date information about the program. There are different recruiters for the different branches of the Armed Services and you can contact any/all of them in your local area. The Medicine and the Military's website has a "Contact a Recruiter" page that lists all of the phone numbers and additional contact information. I recommend visiting the site since it also provides a lot details about the HPSP, including a checklist for applying, and additional information. It is also good to try to speak with alumni from your college or university who are in the HPSP to hear why they chose to do it and what their experiences have been like.

Each year at Johns Hopkins University and later at Franklin & Marshall College, I had several students (both men and women) choose to apply for this program and were accepted. While a few had family members who had served in the Military, many did not. Personality-wise, the students who opted for this choice tended to be highly disciplined and liked an intense team-based culture. While this option isn't for everyone, it can be a good way to emerge from medical school debt-free while also making a difference in the lives of members of the Military and their families. Also, if you are interested in a long-term medical career in the Military, this program is an excellent option.

2. National Health Service Corps (U.S. Department of Health & Human Services)

The Health Resources and Services Administration's Fact Sheet outlines the essentials of this scholarship program, noting: "Students pursuing a career in primary health care are eligible to receive funding for their education in exchange for practicing in rural, urban, and frontier communities with limited access to care, upon graduation and licensure."[5] In exchange for having your tuition and fees covered and receiving a small stipend, you will owe time working at a National Health Service Corps site (a 1-year service commitment for every year of medical school funded by the NHSC). This is a competitive program; in 2017, the NHSC received 2,068 applications and awarded 181 scholarships.[6]

Since this scholarship is for students who plan to pursue a career in a primary care specialty (including areas such as pediatrics, family medicine, internal medicine), you must be very sure that's what you will go into. If you reach the end of medical school and choose a non-primary care specialty, you are then subject to the consequences of breaching the NHSC Scholarship Program Contract. This includes being "liable to the United States for repayment of all NHSC SP funds paid to them and to the school on their behalf. The amount owed must be paid in full within three (3) years of the date of default."[7]

Scholarships at Individual Medical Schools

Many medical schools offer scholarships ranging from a few thousand dollars to full tuition. The Financial Aid page of their website generally lists the scholarships available and whether applicants are automatically considered or need to submit a separate application. It is worth getting to know about these options because some are open to incoming students whereas you can apply for others after your first year or beyond.

Scholarships awarded by Outside Organizations

There are numerous scholarship search engines online. Fastweb is one of them. It contains listings representing professional associations, individual charities and programs, and other sources of scholarship money. Some of the scholarships have very narrow criteria (for example, being a student from a specific geographic area) so read through the listings carefully.

Also, check the Financial Aid pages of medical school websites since many of them list external scholarship resources. Georgetown University School of Medicine's Financial Aid website[8] is a good example of how medical schools share resources to help students figure out how to finance their education. You can speak with the Financial Aid office as well, especially if you have any questions about how outside scholarships may impact your aid.

Loans

For many of you, the reality is that you will need to take out loans to pay for medical school. There are three main sources to consider: Federal/State loans, loans through your medical school, and private loans. Once you see your financial aid package, you can assess which loans are the best option for you. The Financial Aid office at your medical school generally provides information about these options or you can also consult resources such as the AAMC's FIRST (Financial Information, Resources, Services, and Tools) program. On their website, they note that this program "provides free resources to help you make wise financial decisions. Whether you're thinking about how to afford medical school, applying for student loans, or determining your loan repayment options, you'll find unbiased, reliable guidance from FIRST."[9]

Loan Repayment/Forgiveness Programs

Federal level

According to the U.S. Department of Education's Federal Student Aid website, "Public Service Loan Forgiveness (PSLF) Program forgives the remaining balance on your Direct Loans after you have made 120 qualifying monthly payments under a qualifying repayment plan while working full-time for a qualifying employer."[10] This means that in ten years, whatever loan debt you have (as long as it's through a Direct Loan) would be eliminated. There are very specific rules for this program and it requires an application with employer certification once you reach the 120 payments threshold. Also, since this is a federal program, it is subject to change or elimination depending on congressional action.

State level

A number of states have incentive programs to encourage medical students to go into primary care. If you work at a nonprofit hospital or clinic for a set period of time (for example, ten years), they will "forgive" or repay a set amount of your loans. A list of these states and more information about the Loan Forgiveness programs they offer is available on the National Health Service Corps website.[11]

Financing medical school is not the most uplifting topic but since it is a reality you will have to deal with, it is better to be prepared and informed about your options. This way, you will be better able to decide what course of action is best for you.

· CHAPTER NINETEEN ·

PREPARING FOR WHAT LIES AHEAD IN MEDICAL SCHOOL

Medicine is changing rapidly and new insights are emerging constantly. Medical school is just the beginning of your training and you will always have to keep up to date on new developments. In addition to earning your initial board certification in your specialty, medical specialties now require you to recertify every 8-10 years as well as accumulate a specific amount of Continuing Medical Education credits (usually on an annual basis). If you are not a person who enjoys learning new things all the time, then medicine may not be right for you.

It is important to understand what actually happens in medical school. Many of my advisees over the years have admitted that they didn't really know much about the curriculum, board exams, clinical rotations, and applying for residency programs. They just knew that they had to get into medical school as the first step towards becoming a doctor. Knowing what lies ahead in medical school will help you gain a better understand of why we are recommending how to develop specific academic skills and how they will be useful to you when you are in medical school.

First 2 Years - Pre-Clinical

During your first 2 years of medical school, you will be getting a foundation in the science of the human body. It's important to know that different medical schools have different approaches to teaching subjects including biochemistry, pharmacology, and other topics. They also vary in how they teach anatomy and physiology as well as when/how they have you work on cadavers (bodies you dissect). Some medical schools have a block curriculum where you will focus on one organ system at a time and learn everything about normal and abnormal functions. At others, students take multiple courses at the same time.

Teaching methods also vary. For example, problem based learning (PBL) is becoming increasingly popular. This is when you would be part of a small team of about 8 medical students guided by faculty facilitators. You would be introduced to 1-2 medical cases that you would then work through as a group. Other medical schools feature a more traditional lecture-based curriculum and some are a hybrid between PBL and lectures.

Additionally, almost all medical schools now have courses in the first two years where you will start building your communication skills with patients. Often this will start with you interacting with standardized patients, who are essentially actors who portray different conditions. You may also work with advanced patient simulators, robots who are able to simulate breathing, have a heartbeat, and enable you to practice in a no risk environment. Your interactions are often recorded then played back and a faculty member will discuss your performance.

Grading has changed in recent times and many medical schools have moved to a Pass/Fail system for your first two years. This is to encourage collaboration with your fellow students rather than competition and also to get you to focus on learning the material rather than being solely focused on your grades. Some schools do still have a letter grading system while others that have a Pass/Fail system may do a class rank. These are good details to find out during the application process.

At the end of your second year, you will take Step 1 of the United States Medical Licensing Exam (USMLE). According to the USMLE website, Step 1 is "divided into seven 60-minute blocks and administered in one 8-hour testing session. The number of questions per block on a given examination form may vary, but will not exceed 40. The total number of items on the overall examination form will not exceed 280."[1] Your score on this exam is a key factor in how competitive you will be for different residency training programs (when you will get training in your specialized field of medicine).

Year 3 & 4 - Clinical Rotations

After successfully passing Step 1, you will begin your clinical rotations. These are also referred to as clerkships. All medical students have to complete specific rotations including specialties like psychology, obstetrics/gynecology, and then often have some freedom to choose clinical rotations in other specialties. Here again, you will find differences between medical schools. Some will have you complete specialties in 8-10 week blocks whereas others will have you doing several hours a week of multiple specialties and build in time where you can gain exposure to other specialties.

In each of these rotations, you will be evaluated. This often takes the form of grades or a High Pass, Pass, Fail system. Supervising attending physicians also offer specific written feedback on how you did. These evaluations will also factor into residency applications.

During the fall of your 4th year, you will apply for and interview at residency programs. Then, in the spring, you will submit your ranked list of programs where you interviewed. They will also be submitted a ranked list of applicants. On Match Day in March, you will find out where you will be doing your residency training. That summer (usually in late June/early July), you will start your residency program and begin gaining the foundation in your medical specialty area. The length of your training depends on the specialty. Pediatrics, internal medicine, and others will generally be 3 years whereas surgery can be as long as 7 years. As you now see, getting into medical school is just the very beginning and that the sooner you start developing your academic skills, the better!

Having a deep love of learning will be an asset throughout your time as a medical student and in every step of your career.

Following your curiosity and being interested in learning new information will help you both professionally and personally. Being up to date on the latest medical breakthroughs is important but also understanding current events, cultural backgrounds, and other knowledge can make all the difference when working with patients and colleagues. Try to make time to read articles or books. Another popular option is to listen to podcasts or audiobooks. Choose whatever technique works best for you.

Learning a new skill can also be helpful. Maybe you have always wanted to learn how to play the ukulele...watch some YouTube videos and do it! One student decided to teach herself how to bake all kinds of cookies and other desserts and share them with other students in her college house. Talk about a delicious way to de-stress! Picking up something fun and new is a good stress reliever and keeps life interesting.

Be aware of the physical and emotional demands you will face in medical school and as a doctor.

So many pre-meds exclusively focus on the intellectual/academic demands and completely forget to think about the other demanding aspects of medicine and whether they can handle them. Depending on your specialty, you may be standing for long periods of time, or looking through a microscope for hours a day. Surgeons especially have to be very focused for hours on end during an operation and don't run out for bathroom breaks or to take a phone call. Since you will begin practicing your clinical skills very early on in medical school, it is good to start preparing for the physical parts of the medicine.

You also need to be cognizant of the emotional aspect of medicine. It is often under recognized but is one of the major sources of physician burnout. In medical school and then depending on your specialty, you will see patients die and in some cases, they will die because of something you did or did not do. In other cases, you will have done everything humanly possible and they still die. How do you think you will handle this?

Also, while you want to cultivate a good working relationship with your patients, you also have to maintain a certain amount of emotional distance so that you can provide them with care that is not biased by your feelings. You are not your patient's friend although you can be close with them and their families. At the end of the day, you need to be able to turn off and not constantly be thinking and worrying about your patients. Some physicians find this just isn't possible for them and they have to decide whether to continue on in practice or shift to another area such as medical journal editing, hospital administration, or another field. A wonderful doctor I got to know is a perfect example of this. After years of being a pediatric ER physician, she found she couldn't stop thinking about what happened to the children after she treated them and they were either discharged or admitted to the hospital. Many of the kids were victims of domestic violence and the doctor worried about what would happen to them. Over time, this stress and worry built up and began affecting her health. She decided to become the medical editor of a website that provides critical information for parents and kids, a great way to continue helping patients.

Make sure to get enough sleep, eat foods that nourish your body and mind, and exercise on a consistent basis so that you stay healthy.

Unfortunately, physician burnout, depression, addiction issues, and even suicide are on the rise. The National Academy of Medicine featured an article called "Breaking the Culture of Silence on Physician Suicide" in which they share: "Every year an estimated 400 U.S. physicians take their lives. Numerous global studies involving every medical and surgical specialty indicate that approximately 1 in 3 physicians is experiencing burnout at any given time."[2] Given that most medical schools have an incoming class of around 150 students, that means that every year, the equivalent of two and a half classes commit suicide. A December 2016 article in the Journal of the American Medical Association notes that "the overall prevalence of depression or depressive symptoms among medical students was 27.2%, and the overall prevalence of suicidal ideation was 11.1%."[3] I share these statistics not to scare you but to raise your awareness that the pressure cooker of a career in medicine means it is extremely important to take care of yourself. Think about how much you want to help your patients and then realize that you won't be able to help any of them if your health is compromised. Having healthy habits will go a long way to making sure you are at your best for your patients.

Medical school is an exciting next step towards becoming a doctor since you finally get to delve deeper into the science of the human body and begin to interact with patients. Early on during your first year (or even right when you start), your school will have a White Coat Ceremony. This is where you will literally put on your white coat, signifying you are officially starting your medical training. While you know you have many years of hard work ahead, savor this moment and realize the dedication you have put in to get there!

CHAPTER TWENTY

OTHER CAREER OPTIONS

For a variety of reasons, you may be thinking about other careers and may ultimately choose to pursue one instead of medicine. There are many rewarding and fascinating careers in healthcare as well as at the intersection of healthcare and other fields. Here are some factors to consider and ideas for exploring different careers.

As you think about other careers, pinpoint the areas of being a doctor that appealed to you.

Being able to evaluate the specific elements of a career in medicine that drew you to it will help you decide what other path(s) you want to consider. For example, if the main reason you wanted to become a doctor is to help children by treating their medical conditions, then you may want to consider a related health career. If what attracted you to medicine was being on the cutting edge of breakthroughs in healthcare, then you can consider fields like clinical or translational research or public health. Identifying these areas can then help you look for similar traits in other careers.

If you are considering a different career in healthcare, think about how much (or little) interaction you want to have with patients.

There is a spectrum when it comes to careers and the amount of patient interaction they have. On one end of the spectrum are people whose sole focus is on the science of the human body and they do not interact with patients at all. For example, a pathologist assistant helps the pathologist with autopsies, sections pieces of tissue, and does critical work but they do not talk to patients at any point. In the middle are people who have some patient contact but again, are not constantly speaking with patients. For example, a nurse anesthetist may speak with a patient before and after surgery and will spend time with the patient throughout surgery but at that point, the patient is under anesthesia. On the other end of the spectrum are people who are constantly speaking with patients. These include primary care physician assistants and nurses, physical therapists, dentists, and many other healthcare professionals.

Consider the scope of practice each health profession encompasses.

Each health profession has its own core responsibilities and roles. As a physician assistant, you can often have a fairly high degree of autonomy but overall, you are still supervised by a physician. Both the individual place you work as well as the state in which it is located may dictate your scope of practice, in other words what you can and can't do. For example, as a PA or NP, you may be able to write prescriptions in some states but not others. Also, the degree of independence you have in terms of diagnosing and treating patients will vary. This is important to think about when considering PA and/or nursing as a potential profession.

If you like being able to design your own treatment protocols for patients and getting to spend more time with them, then physical or occupational therapy might be a good choice. Both of these fields have many opportunities for specialization but at their core, they both involve spending a lot of time with each patient. Some physical therapists and occupational therapists may spend up to an hour or even more per patient.

Another field growing in demand is genetic counseling. Several alumni I spoke with who had initially been pre-med switched to this field after shadowing both MDs and genetic counselors. This field is not only about prenatal testing and counseling; it includes areas such as cancer genetics and others. Genetic counselors are also often involved in clinical research. The degree required is a Master of Science in Genetic Counseling.

If you enjoy research, consider applying to master's or doctoral programs at medical schools.

Many people don't know that medical schools generally have graduate degree programs other than the MD. Degree fields include Genetics/Genomics, Biomedical Engineering, Immunology, and many others. Often degrees at the PhD level are fully funded. You would be preparing for a research career that can involve a high degree of interaction with clinicians. Translational research ("bench to bedside") can be a very collaborative, fascinating career.

If you like an interdisciplinary approach to the healthcare field, consider careers in public health.

While you may have heard of public health, it is easy to think of it as just health education or one other specific area. While medicine is the practice of examining and caring for the health of an individual tree (a patient), public health is at the forest level. Public health is an incredible umbrella under which many specialty areas reside. The Association of Schools and Programs of Public Health (ASPPH) lists the following definition: "Public health protects and improves the health of individuals, families, communities, and populations, locally and globally."[1] They list some of the different areas you can focus on including Behavioral and Social Science, Biostatistics and Informatics, Community Health, Environmental Health, Epidemiology, Global Health, Health Policy and Management, Health Promotion and Communication, Maternal and Child Health, and Minority Health and Health Disparities. You can pursue graduate degrees at the Master's level (the most common of these is the Master of Public Health - MPH) or the doctoral level, leading to either a PhD or a DrPH (Doctor of Public Health). Many medical students and physicians are opting to pursue an MPH as a dual degree so that they have the foundation in this important topic.

Research different health careers so you can really understand their similarities and differences and make an informed decision about what is right for you.

I think the most comprehensive resource for learning more about other health careers including information about scope of practice, degree needed, and additional information is ExploreHealthCareers.org. Members of the Federation of Associations of Schools of the Health Professions (FASHP) partner with Liaison International (the company that powers the site) and this ensures the content is up to date for each of the health professions featured on the site.[2] Features including questions on whether a health career is right for you, a "Find Your Fit" tool, and resources on building your career are extremely helpful. I encourage you to take a look at this site.

Professional associations also have excellent resources. For example, if you were interested in becoming a vet, you could visit the websites for the Association of American Veterinary Medical Colleges and the American Veterinary Medical Association. If you have more than one health profession in mind, you can search for and view the sites for each school association.

If you are interested in both healthcare and other fields, consider positions at the intersection of these fields.

Let's say you always were fascinated by both medicine and business. Think about all of the wearable devices out there that people are using to track different elements of their health. Those had to be researched, developed, and tested before they were manufactured. Marketing campaigns had to be created as well as other ways to connect with consumers. The point is that there are so many opportunities that can combine your interests.

Another great example of this is public policy. If you have an interest in government, economics, or subjects along those lines as well as an interest in healthcare, then working for a think tank, consulting firm, non-profit, or other organization could be a great fit. You could be on the front lines of impacting healthcare policy and legislation and helping thousands of people.

Talk to people both in healthcare careers and other fields.

Interview people about their career path and the decisions they have made. Alumni from your college/university are great to talk to as well as people in your community. When you speak with them, ask them about when they were in your shoes as a student trying to decide on their future. Were they considering other careers? How did they decide to pursue the career they ended up selecting? What do they think of this now? What do they love about their current job and what would they change? Often, hearing about others' experiences can be very helpful and may change the way you look at your career options.

Keep in mind that you can always pursue one career for some time and then if medicine still really calls to you, you can still pursue that path in the future.

Your first job after college will not be your last nor does it lock you into a certain path. The door to medicine is still open even if you choose to go in a different direction initially. If you do decide to become a physician and it has been a while (five years or more) since you have taken the prerequisite courses or if you never took them, then considering a career-changer post baccalaureate program would be a good idea. Take a look at that section earlier on in this book for more information about these types of programs and important factors to keep in mind.

SUCCESS STORIES & FIVE FINAL TIPS

We both hope that part of what you are taking away from this book is that you don't have to be a pre-med robot or clone. You are unique and even if you follow exactly what someone else did (the same grades, MCAT score, activities, etc.), it may not get you the outcome you want. Medical schools have excellent bullshit detectors and see right through applicants who did the pre-med version of paint-by-numbers. You still need a body of work that gives them evidence you are academically prepared and have the core competencies needed to succeed in medical school but what that looks like can be very different for each applicant. In this chapter, we wanted to highlight the uniqueness of multiple people who are now at various stages in their medical career (medical school, residency, and out in practice). We hope these profiles demonstrate that carving your own path is important and give you confidence that you can still do activities that are meaningful to you and they can help you become a better applicant.

The Expert Juggler

I'm not talking about someone who juggled a lot of activities. I am literally referring to the fact this person taught himself how to juggle. One day, E.J. was bored, Googled "Things to do when you're bored" and juggling came up. He started small, with a few balls, and then as he got better, progressed to harder items. At one point, he even juggled knives (not recommended for premeds!). While you may not think juggling has anything to do with medicine, it was the process E.J. took that encapsulates who he is. He was curious about something, tried it and recognized that being able to move from the beginner stage to being more advanced would require a lot of work and practice, he then put in that work and practice, and became really good.

E.J. majored in Math but also loves languages. He studied Chinese, Arabic, and other languages but really liked Russian. E.J. ended up studying abroad in Russia, taking math classes and immersing himself in the culture. He used his love of math by volunteering with a community organization where he helped local residents prepare their tax returns. He did an interesting internship with a public health department in a major city, helping them design a better way to deal with mosquitos. After college, E.J. joined National Health Corps and again used a love of math and technology to implement a system for a local health clinic. He wrote one of my favorite personal statements of all time - it was about working with undocumented immigrants in a clinic, the strong connections he built with these patients, and the insight he gained about what is broken about our healthcare system and how it could be fixed. E.J. got accepted to multiple medical schools and is now happily using juggling as an outlet for the pressures of medical school.

The Scuba Diver

S.D. is a great example of how your research interests do not have to be clinical in nature and that sometimes those experiences help you clarify what you want to do. After earning her scuba diving certification as a teenager, S.D. wanted to study marine biology in more depth during college. She spent a summer doing full-time research in the Florida Keys as part of an internship with the Florida Fish and Wildlife Commission. She learned a lot through that experience, sharing: "My job involved working with biologists to restore Florida's native Conch population. Though the biologists were inspiring, they lacked equipment and their research was underfunded. Their boats would often break down and take weeks to repair. We spent most days in seclusion, either scuba diving many miles from shore, or working alone in the lab. I quickly learned that the life of a marine biologist could be frustrating and isolated...I particularly missed working with people."

S.D. started her college career at one university and then transferred to another. She worked at a local flower shop and also spent time volunteering at a hospital as well as shadowing physicians there. Getting to work closely with people and help them was very meaningful for S.D. and helped her decide medicine was the right career for her. She was accepted to multiple DO schools, then got off of the waitlist at an MD school that was in state, and chose to attend that school. After excelling in medical school and the first two years of her residency program, S.D. is now Chief Resident.

The Neuroscience Scholar

N.S. is fascinated by the brain and chose to major in Neuroscience. He spent a semester studying abroad in Budapest in a program that was devoted to cognitive science. N.S. also spent time engaging in clinical research at an academic medical center. Studying the brain in all its complexity and nuance made him so happy that when you talked to him about it, he had the biggest smile and just lit up.

N.S. is passionate about learning in general. An example of this is when he attended an event I sponsored where I brought guest speakers in to talk about diabetes. The first panelist asked the audience, "What year was insulin invented?" N.S. raised his hand and gave the correct year. The panelist was extremely impressed since this was not common knowledge and after the event, she asked N.S. how he knew that date. He replied that when he saw the topic of the event, he wanted to learn more and do some prep work prior to attending so that he could get the most out of the event.

Helping others, especially young men of color, become empowered and grow as leaders is one of N.S.'s core values. As a person of color himself, N.S. had a lifetime of experiences of discrimination and what it feels like to be at an economic disadvantage relative to his peers. He mentored other students (both his peers and younger students in the community) and did everything he could to lift up other people. N.S. is flourishing in medical school and continuing to mentor pre-med students of color.

The Crusader for Women and Babies

C.W.B. has always been passionate about maternal and child health. She gained her first exposure to neonatal care during a shadowing experience in middle school and it was a life-changing experience. Throughout college, she spent countless hours at the Labor and Delivery Suite and Neonatal Intensive Care Unit at a local hospital. C.W.B. also completed an in-depth research study comparing the health of mothers and babies in Baltimore with those living in Pune, India. Additionally, she volunteered with the March of Dimes organization for many years and served in a leadership role at the national level during college. She also organized her fellow students to raise funds for this organization.

C.W.B. was also a leader in many areas of campus life. This student and I co-founded an organization dedicated to empowering women seeking to enter the health professions. Additionally, she was Co-Captain of an all-women Indian fusion dance team and engaged in service through organizations including the Ronald McDonald House.

C.W.B. thrived in medical school and in keeping with her passion of caring for mothers and babies, she became an OB/GYN. She is working hard to ensure that infants and their mothers receive the care they need, regardless of their background.

FIVE FINAL TIPS

TIP 1: Your journey as a pre-med, the phases of your medical training, and then your career as a physician are marathons, not sprints.

Winston Churchill famously said, "Now this is not the end. It is not even the beginning of the end. But it is, perhaps, the end of the beginning." The same wisdom applies to medical school. Getting in is the end of the beginning of your journey. You will have your four years of college, 4 years of medical school, and then, depending on what specialty you choose, 3-7 years of residency. Many physicians choose to do a fellowship and then finally, you will be out in practice as a doctor. So, let's say you are 23 when you start medical school, 27 when you graduate, and then you complete a 3 year pediatric residency program, and a year-long fellowship in gastroenterology. That means you will be 31 when you are out in practice. Since many physicians continue to work well into their sixties and even seventies, you will likely have a 30 to 40 year career. While you need to plan for every step of your career as separate marathons and build up your endurance, while you are in each phase, take it one day at a time just as you would run one mile at a time. Consistency is important as is keeping yourself healthy.

TIP 2: This is your future career...own it.

If you are really serious about becoming a doctor, you will do what it takes to make that goal happen. No one else is going to get you into medical school. You are in the driver's seat, which is both exciting and maybe a bit scary. It is good to check in with yourself and keep yourself accountable. Are your actions consistent with your goals? If they are, that's great but if they aren't, then it is time to make changes to get back on track.

TIP 3: Be a fierce advocate for yourself, just as you will be for your patients.

If a person or policy was negatively impacting your patients, what would you do? Chances are, you would fight to get answers and changes made on your patients' behalf. There are times where you may need to stand up for yourself in this same way. For example, you may need to change academic advisors or push to get summer experience funding. Becoming informed about the steps to follow and then taking action is up to you to do.

TIP 4: Know when to ask for help.

No one is exceptional at everything all the time. When you are struggling, reach out and seek people who can assist you. Many students often express concern that if they ask for help, others will think they are not as intelligent or that they are weak. Imagine if you weren't sure about how to do a certain procedure the chief resident asks you to do and instead of asking questions, you did it and harmed a patient. You need to become comfortable asking questions without judging yourself or beating yourself up.

TIP 5: Enjoy the journey.

While the path to medical school is long and often takes unexpected twists and turns, it is also exhilarating. I will never forget how one student's face lit up as she described observing brain surgery right alongside the neurosurgeon performing the procedure. As she told me about each of the steps of the multi-hour surgery, I could see how her goal of becoming a physician had gone from something on the horizon to a true calling she was willing to dedicate everything to achieve. While the 2 am study sessions of Organic Chemistry may drain you and the hours pipetting samples in the lab seem tedious, it will all add up to a collection of experiences you will be proud of and that medical school admissions officers will take note of in your application.

When you become a doctor, you will be caring for someone's mother, father, spouse, partner, sister, brother, or child. That responsibility will be a source of joy when you see your patients recover, a source of sadness when you did everything you could but your patient lost their battle with their illness, and sometimes a source of bewilderment and frustration when you can't definitively diagnose a patient's condition. While you think about that day in the future, don't forget to make the most of today. Your white coat is waiting for you...you just need to step up and do what it takes to claim it. We both wish you all the best for the amazing road ahead!

FOR PARENTS

Is medicine the right career for your child?

You may have seen your daughter or son express an interest in becoming a doctor or you may feel it would be a great career for them. Given the length of training, demands of the career, cost to attend medical school, and many other factors, either your child or you just thinking it would be a good fit is not enough. Your child needs to gain exposure to the medical profession, see whether they both are good at and like challenging coursework in the sciences and humanities, and are willing to devote up to a decade of training beyond their undergraduate years. Providing support and encouragement as they test out whether medicine is the right career for them is the most effective parenting approach. We have both seen people who were essentially pushed or even forced by their parents to become doctors and in many cases, this leads to very negative outcomes.

What to be ready for

If your child has thoroughly explored whether medicine is the right career for them and is now actively working on becoming a strong applicant or is in the application process, both they and you will face new challenges. This is going to be one of the most difficult processes your child has been through in their life so far and it will take a toll on even the toughest students and highest achievers. You need to be prepared for tearful phone calls and Facetime sessions, sad texts, and other expressions of anguish from your child. This is when just being a shoulder for them to cry on and for them to feel like they can vent to is really important.

One of the most important facts to understand is that going straight from college to medical school is now the exception, not the rule. According to the Association of American Medical Colleges' 2018 Matriculating Student Questionnaire, over 63% of entering medical students had taken at least a year between college and medical school.[1] Chapter 4 addresses this topic in much greater depth and I encourage you to read it so that you can learn more about this.

You also need to know going into this process that not everyone gains admission to medical school the first time they apply or in some cases, ever. Even if your child (and you) think they have what it takes and they think they are a good applicant, only about 43% of applicants in any given year matriculate to medical school. There isn't shame in not getting in but it does mean taking a hard look at the weaknesses that led to your child not gaining admission in their first application cycle and then making sure they address those prior to reapplying. Reapplicants can gain admission to medical school but only if they demonstrate they made significant progress in the areas in which they needed improvement.

Your role(s)

As a parent, you can decide which of the following role(s) best suits you and your child. Every child is different and may respond to you taking on one role more than another. You can experiment and see what works for you. Also, it may be that your role(s) will shift depending on where your child is in the preparation or application phase for medical school.

Coach

You can help your child as they work to become a competitive applicant and then get through each phase of the application process. The key is to remember that your child should be in the driver's seat for this process, not you. Also, make sure to not go from coaching/encouraging to badgering or pressuring. Your child is likely putting a huge amount of pressure on her/himself and if you add more to this, you risk negatively affecting your child's performance.

Connector

Remember that at your child's college/university, there are a number of resources they can tap into. They have a faculty academic advisor, a pre-health advisor, and others on campus who can help them. It is important to know when to refer your child to seek guidance rather than trying to do it on your own.

Cheerleader

Ideally, your child would take full ownership of this process and you would just be in the role of supporting and encouraging them.

STRATEGIES FOR SPECIFIC FAMILY BACKGROUNDS

If your child is the first in your family to apply to medical school

Having worked with many students who are first gen pre-meds, I recognize that it is daunting for both the students and parents since there is no frame of reference for this process. As a parent, getting yourself up to speed on what your child needs to do as a pre-med and what the medical school application process is like will help you feel more confident and in the know. Reading the website for your child's college/university pre-health advising office is a good place to start as are the resources listed in the Appendix of this book. If, after gaining that background, you have questions, you can contact your child's pre-health advisor.

If you are a physician

Having been a pre-med yourself, successfully navigating the application process, and then going through the different phases of training to become a doctor, it is tempting to feel you are an expert on this process. The reality is that being a pre-med today, the current admissions process, and medical school have changed dramatically even in the past several years. Unless you are currently serving on a medical school admissions committee and/or interviewing applicants, your knowledge of the process and what it takes to gain admission may not be current. As a result, trying to advise your child on topics like MCAT prep, how many schools to apply to, and other topics will not serve them well. This is where your child's pre-med advisor will be able to provide them with guidance and targeted support.

The area in which you can advise them and help them is in facilitating connections with other physicians. In fact, when medical schools see that one or more of an applicant's parents is a physician but that applicant is light on clinical experience, this can negatively impact an applicant. It is fine for your child to shadow you but you will not be able to write them a letter of recommendation. Introducing them to your colleagues and then having them shadow these physicians is a tangible step you can take that will benefit your child.

Your Child's Pre-med Advisor

Most colleges and universities have a pre-health advising office where your child can receive guidance on every phase of the medical school application process. There are often individual advising appointments, drop-in hours, programs, online resources, and many more ways that these offices support students. Mentioning this to your child and recommending they schedule an appointment or attend drop-in hours is a helpful step you can take.

If you call or email your child's pre-med advisor asking specific questions about your child, the advisor will likely not be able to discuss these details with you because of a federal law called the Family Educational Rights and Privacy Act (FERPA). Your child would need to provide written authorization to the advisor in order for them to discuss any academic or personal matters with you as the parent. It's often best to just have a conversation with your child about how they are doing and what they are working on rather than trying to discuss this with their advisor. I did occasionally hold advising sessions that included both the student and parent(s) so that everyone was on the same page but this is not something that every advisor or college/university may offer.

Parent Do's and Don'ts

Do...

- Provide emotional support for your child

- Educate yourself on the different phases of the application process

- Understand the pre-med advising services your child's college/university provides and encourage your child to tap into those resources

Don't...

- Push your child to become a physician if they do not want to

- Take the lead in your child's pre-med journey and/or application process

- Call medical schools on behalf of your child or show up at interviews (yes, this actually happens!)

Dr. Kirby's Diagnosis: Tips for Parents

Parents play a very important part in the success of the pre-med student. The role of the parents changes from high school to college. In high school, the role of the parent(s) is to help the student with general development as a young adult with emphasis on all phases of life. In the application to college process, the role of the parent begins to change to a more collaborative one with the student taking the lead in the choice of which college to attend. In college, the role of the parent shifts to a more supportive and advisory role to help the student succeed independently. The ability of parents to perform these different roles can greatly aid in the successful transition from high school student to a competitive and successful pre-med student.

High School

Education in high school will consist of the student's classwork and extracurricular activities. It is important to identify any weaknesses that exist in fundamental subjects and address the problems immediately. The goal should be to develop good skills in a variety of subjects. During the school year, the student's education can be expanded by going to local lectures on different subjects such as art, politics or finance. Participation in school plays, or clubs can be an excellent way for students to gain confidence and communication skills. Short term classes are often available at local colleges or museums that can give the student a low pressure exposure to a variety of different subjects while interacting with a diverse group of students of different ages and backgrounds.

Summers can be a particularly good time to gain diverse knowledge through experiences. Independent travel to attend a variety of programs in different areas of the country can provide useful experiences along with a better sense of what kind of community the student feels comfortable in for college. If the student has to work, those experiences can give the benefits of a sound work ethic and exposure to a variety of different people. All of these experiences will provide the student with the opportunity to connect with mentors and to develop a network of people who share their interests and goals.

It is important for your child to exercise regularly and be aware of healthy nutrition. Exercise can take the form of team or individual sports, including classes such as karate, Pilates, yoga or dance. Team sports give the benefit of learning to work with others toward a shared goal. Individual sports have the benefits of learning self-motivation and discipline. In combination with exercise the student should learn about nutrition and a healthy diet. Through this, the student will hopefully experience the long-term positive effects of feeling healthy and incorporate this into their daily life. Having these healthy habits will be very useful during the stressful years of college, medical school and beyond.

Parents need to discuss the appropriate use of social media with their child. While the internet and social media have many positive aspects, they also have negative aspects that can harm the student. The student needs to be aware that colleges will look at their social media pages and the content can be a determining factor in whether a student is accepted or not.

Try to teach your child how to make good decisions. Discuss difficult situations that arise and possible solutions so they can develop problem-solving skills that can be used in college and in life. Hopefully you can teach them that daily good decisions about all aspects of life are the key to long-term success. The more of these things your student becomes proficient at, the better chance they have to succeed in college and become a successful pre-med.

The final part of the high school experience is the choice of college. Hopefully by senior year you will have a good appreciation of your child's strengths and weaknesses and a sense of what environment they would thrive in. When you visit a college observe how comfortable your child is and if it is a good match for their ability. Particularly for pre-meds the student has to start off college successfully from Day One. Having to adjust to an uncomfortable living situation or an uncomfortable learning environment can hurt your child's chances from the start. The wrong choice of school can end a pre-med student's career before it starts. The whole process will give you a chance to transition your relationship as the student takes the lead in the college decision process. Hopefully this will be the basis for your transition to a positive supportive and advisory role during college.

College

Your role as a parent in college changes to a supportive advisory role so that you can be helpful when needed. We outline the challenges of college for the student in that section of the book and familiarity with those issues will be useful to parents. One particularly problematic area for parents, especially those who are doctors, is assuming that the way college was for them is still the case now. Parents need to understand that college is very different now than when they were students. The whole approach to education has changed in the electronic information era. Assignments, tests, and teaching styles have all changed. For pre-meds, the MCAT has changed substantially as have the required courses and expectations for extracurricular activities. I have learned a lot from discussions with Kirsten about what the current student goes through and recognize how different it was from my experience. Don't assume that you know the demands on the present-day student unless you have actual exposure to the current college experience.

It is important for parents to encourage their children to be advocates for themselves. Hopefully the groundwork for this was done during high school. You can certainly help by talking through different subjects to enable your child to clarify their thoughts and plans but they should fight their own battles. Parents that directly interact with advisors or professors can hurt their child in several ways. Most importantly, the student doesn't develop the interpersonal skills crucial for them to successfully handle difficult situations. In addition, the parents can create an adversarial relationship with the academic team that can ultimately hurt their child. It is very difficult as a parent to see your child struggling but in most cases the best thing is for them to work things out with your assistance as needed.

One of the hardest things for students and parents to come to grips with is that the student may not be a competitive pre-med in the traditional manner. This can be for a variety of different reasons that we discussed in other chapters. If the student has the ability but has not been able to create a competitive undergraduate resume, then additional education in a post-baccalaureate pre-med program or graduate school can make the student more competitive. If on the other hand, the student seems not to be a competitive applicant and is committed to a career in healthcare there are many other excellent career options. As a pathologist, I employ pathology assistants who have attended a masters program where they trained to do dissections and perform autopsies. They are a critical part of my practice and we work together as a team. Other examples include medical and surgical assistants who work as part of the medical team seeing and treating patients. In these and other alternative fields, the student can have a fulfilling and financially rewarding career in healthcare.

In summary, you have the opportunity as a parent to teach good life skills in high school that will enable your child to successfully compete as a pre-med in college. Hopefully you can develop a relationship that will enable you to support your child so that together you can celebrate their success.

ACKNOWLEDGEMENTS

Kirsten Kirby

This book is the realization of a lifelong goal and I have many people I want to thank:

All of the pre-health students and alumni I have advised over the years: You are amazing and you continue to inspire me every day. It was a privilege to work with you.

Dr. J. Matthew Neal – Getting to work with you at The American College of Physicians was an honor. Our conversations about writing and your unwavering support and encouragement gave me the confidence to finally write my book. Having you write the Foreword was incredibly meaningful and I can't thank you enough.

Dr. Caroline Kirby – To my talented cousin who is carrying on the family legacy in medicine, thank you for your feedback on this book. I am both proud of and inspired by you.

David Verrier – I was so fortunate to have you as my mentor in health professions advising during my time at Johns Hopkins University and beyond. Thank you for the wisdom you have shared with me over the years and for helping me grow as an advisor.

Chelsea Haring – You are such a powerhouse and wonder woman! Thank you for your suggestions on the book draft and for your friendship.

Rona Shirdan – To my editor extraordinaire and wonderful godmother, I am blessed to have you in my life.

Abbie G., Claire S., and Joy C. – You are amazing women and dear friends. Your words of encouragement kept me going even in tough times.

My mom, Dinah Kirby – Thank you for your willingness to type up dad's portions and for your patience throughout this process. Your love and support were greatly appreciated!

My dad, Dr. William Kirby – We have had these conversations for so many years and we finally are putting this book out in the world. We did it!

My husband, Kieron – Your support of my dreams has meant everything to me. I would not be who I am and where I am without you. I love you so much!

Dr. William Kirby

To my daughter Kirsten – The whole process of producing this book from the years of conversation to the work sessions to producing the final product has been a great experience. Your dedication to helping others is demonstrated through the thoroughness and thoughtfulness of this comprehensive book. I am so proud of you and the book we have produced through your persistent hard work!

To my wife and family – As this book shows, becoming a doctor is challenging and demanding for the individual and his/her family. Thank you for the love and support that made my life and career both possible and successful.

ABOUT THE AUTHORS

Kirsten E. Kirby, M.S.Ed., served as Assistant Director of Pre-Professional Programs and Advising at Johns Hopkins University and later, as Director of Health Professions Advising at Franklin & Marshall College. Having advised students at both an elite research university and a liberal arts college, she understands the unique opportunities and challenges each type of institution presents to pre-meds. Ms. Kirby graduated *magna cum laude* from Smith College and was inducted into Phi Beta Kappa. She earned her Master of Science in Education at University of Pennsylvania.

William M. Kirby, M.D., graduated from Swarthmore College and attended medical school at Penn State University School of Medicine. Dr. Kirby completed his residency training in pathology at Yale University and completed a fellowship at Barnes Hospital. He is now the Associate Chair of Pathology and Chief of the Autopsy Service for the Christiana Care Health System in Delaware.

NOTES

Throughout this book, the following sources are cited. All sources and links were verified on April 24, 2019.

Deciding Whether Medicine Is The Right Career For You

1. Association of American Medical Colleges. MCAT and GPA Grid for Applicants and Acceptees to U.S. Medical Schools, 2017-2018 through 2018-2019. (aggregated) https://www.aamc.org/download/321508/data/factstablea23.pdf

2. Budd, Ken. AAMC News. 7 Ways to Reduce Medical School Debt. https://news.aamc.org/medical-education/article/ 7-ways-reduce-medical-school-debt/

3. University of Pennsylvania Positive Psychology. Authentic Happiness Questionnaire Center. https://www.authentichappiness.sas.upenn.edu/testcenter

4. National Cancer Institute Dictionary of Cancer Terms. https://www.cancer.gov/publications/dictionaries/cancer-terms/def/ allopathic-medicine

5. A.T. Still University. A.T. Still Biography. https://www.atsu.edu/ museum-of-osteopathic-medicine/museum-at-still

6. American Osteopathic Association. What is Osteopathic Manipulative Treatment? https://osteopathic.org/ what-is-osteopathic-medicine/osteopathic-manipulative-treatment/

7. American Association of Colleges of Osteopathic Medicine. What is Osteopathic Medicine?
https://www.aacom.org/become-a-doctor/about-om

8. American Association of Colleges of Osteopathic Medicine. What is Osteopathic Medicine?
https://www.aacom.org/become-a-doctor/about-om

9. American Osteopathic Association. Single GME Student FAQs.
https://osteopathic.org/students/resources/single-gme/single-gme-student-faqs/

10. American Osteopathic Association. Single GME Student FAQs.
https://osteopathic.org/students/resources/single-gme/single-gme-student-faqs/

11. Doctors that DO. https://doctorsthatdo.org/

12. Atul Gawande, MD, MPH. http://atulgawande.com/about/

13. Danielle Ofri, MD. https://danielleofri.com/

14. KevinMD. https://www.kevinmd.com/blog/about-kevin-md

What To Do In High School

1. Association of American Medical Colleges. Medical School Admissions Requirements (BS/MD filter).
https://apps.aamc.org/msar-ui

2. Association of American Medical Colleges. What it's like to participate in a BS/MD program.
https://students-residents.aamc.org/choosing-medical-career/article/what-its-participate-bsmd-program/

Pre-Med Pathway & Timelines For College Students

1. Fu, Melanie Y. and Joung, Jiwon. "More Students Take Time Off Before Applying to Medical School." February 25, 2015. https://www.thecrimson.com/article/2015/2/25/medical-applicants-time-off/

2. Association of American Medical Colleges report: Age of Applicants to U.S. Medical Schools at Anticipated Matriculation by Sex and Race/Ethnicity, 2014-2015 through 2017-2018. https://www.aamc.org/download/321468/data/factstablea6.pdf

3. National Health Corps. Our Mission. http://www.nationalhealthcorps.org/national/our-mission-0

Pre-Med Pathway & Timelines For Career-Changers

1. Association of American Medical Colleges. Table A-6: Age of Applicants to U.S. Medical Schools at Anticipated Matriculation by Sex and Race/Ethnicity, 2014-2015 through 2017-2018. https://www.aamc.org/download/321468/data/factstablea6.pdf

2. Goucher College Post-Bac Pre-med Linkage Opportunities. https://www.goucher.edu/learn/graduate-programs/ post-baccalaureate-premed-program/linkage-to-medical-school

How Medical Schools Will Assess You

1. Pamela Slim. *Body of Work*. 2013. https://pamelaslim.com/books/

2. Association of American Medical Colleges Additional Information about Core Competencies. https://www.aamc.org/admissions/dataandresearch/477184/ additionalinformationoncorecompetencies.html, accessed 3/13/19

3. What Medical Schools are Looking for: Understanding the 15 Core Competencies. https://students-residents.aamc.org/applying-medical-school/article/ med-schools-looking-for-15-competencies/

4. Association of American Medical Colleges. Anatomy of an Applicant. https://students-residents.aamc.org/applying-medical-school/ preparing-med-school/anatomy-applicant/

Why Your Mindset & Relationships Matter

1. National Association of Advisors for the Health Professions. About NAAHP, Inc. and Contact Information. https://www.naahp.org/naahpwwwsite/about-naahp

2. Association of American Medical Colleges Advisor Corner: Preparing for Committee Letter Process. https://students-residents.aamc.org/applying-medical-school/article/advisor-corner-preparing-committee-letter-process/

Research, Clinical, Service, & Other Activities

1. Association of American Medical Colleges. Summer Undergraduate Research Programs. https://students-residents.aamc.org/choosing-medical-career/article/summer-undergraduate-research-programs/

Advice For International Students

1. AAMC Table A-3: Applicants to U.S. Medical Schools by State of Legal Residence, 2009-2010 through 2018-2019. https://www.aamc.org/download/321460/data/factstablea3.pdf

2. AAMC Table A-4: Matriculants to U.S. Medical Schools by State of Legal Residence, 2009-2010 through 2018-2019. https://www.aamc.org/download/321462/data/factstablea4.pdf

3. AAMC Medical School Admissions Requirements. https://apps.aamc.org/msar-ui/#/landing

4. Vanderbilt University School of Medicine. Medical Student Affairs page for International Students. https://medschool.vanderbilt.edu/student-affairs/cim-resources/international-students/

Preparing To Apply

1. Association of American Medical Colleges. Medical School Admissions Requirements. https://apps.aamc.org/msar-ui/#/landing

2. Association of American Medical Colleges. Table A-1: U.S. Medical School Applications and Matriculants by School, State of Legal Residence, and Sex, 2018-2019. https://www.aamc.org/download/321442/data/factstablea1.pdf

3. Washington University School of Medicine in St. Louis. Dis-Orientation Guide. https://sites.wustl.edu/diso201920/

4. AAMC Fee Assistance Program. https://students-residents.aamc.org/applying-medical-school/applying-medical-school-process/fee-assistance-program/

5. Association of American Medical Colleges. How Social Media Can Affect Your Application. https://students-residents.aamc.org/applying-medical-school/article/how-social-media-can-affect-your-application/

6. Leo Babauta. Zen Habits. https://zenhabits.net/

The MCAT

1. The Association of American Medical Colleges. The MCAT Essentials for the Testing Year 2019. https://aamc-orange.global.ssl.fastly.net/production/media/filer_public/ea/55/ea5574b3-c544-4958-87e2-5b6cf7ac6186/essentials_2019_final_02072019.pdf

2. The Association of American Medical Colleges. What's on the MCAT Exam? https://students-residents.aamc.org/mcatexam

Interviewing

1. About CASPer. https://takecasper.com/about-casper/

2. Association of American Medical Colleges Application and Acceptance Protocols for Applicants. https://students-residents.aamc.org/applying-medical-school/article/application-and-acceptance-protocols-applicants/

Acceptances, Waitlists, & Rejections

1. Association of American Medical Colleges Application and Acceptance Protocols for Applicants. https://students-residents.aamc.org/applying-medical-school/article/application-and-acceptance-protocols-applicants/

How To Pay For Medical School

1. Association of American Medical Colleges Tuition and Student Fees Workbook. https://www.aamc.org/data/tuitionandstudentfees/

2. Student Loan Hero. A Look at the Shocking Student Loan Debt Statistics for 2019. https://studentloanhero.com/student-loan-debt-statistics/

3. Zillow. United States Home Prices and Values. https://www.zillow.com/home-values/

4. Department of Defense. Medicine + the Military. https://www.medicineandthemilitary.com/joining-and-eligibility/medical-school-scholarships

5. National Health Service Corps Fact Sheet https://nhsc.hrsa.gov/sites/default/files/NHSC/scholarships/nhsc-scholarship-fact-sheet.pdf

6. National Health Service Corps Scholarship Program. School Year 2019-2020 Application and Program Guide. Anticipated Awards. (p. 10) https://nhsc.hrsa.gov/sites/default/files/NHSC/scholarships/nhsc-scholarship-application-program-guidance.pdf

7. National Health Service Corps Scholarship Program. School Year 2019-2020 Application and Program Guide. Breach of Contract (pg. 39). https://nhsc.hrsa.gov/sites/default/files/NHSC/scholarships/nhsc-scholarship-application-program-guidance.pdf

8. Georgetown University School of Medicine Office of Medical Student Financial Services. Outside Scholarships and Resources. https://som.georgetown.edu/prospectivestudents/financialaid/resources

9. Association of American Medical Colleges. Financial Information, Resources, Services, and Tools (FIRST). https://students-residents.aamc.org/financial-aid/

10. U.S. Department of Education Federal Student Aid Public Service Loan Forgiveness Program. https://studentaid.ed.gov/sa/repay-loans/forgiveness-cancellation/public-service

11. National Health Service Corps Loan Repayment - Determine State Loan Repayment Program Eligibility and Application Requirements. https://nhsc.hrsa.gov/loan-repayment/state-loan-repayment-program/application-requirements.html

Preparing For What Lies Ahead In Medical School

1. United States Medical Licensing Exam Step 1. https://www.usmle.org/step-1/

2. Kishore, S., D. E. Dandurand, A. Mathew, and D. Rothenberger. 2016. Breaking the Culture of Silence on Physician Suicide. *NAM Perspectives.* Discussion Paper, National Academy of Medicine, Washington, DC. https://nam.edu/breaking-the-culture-of-silence-on-physician-suicide/

3. Rotenstein LS, Ramos MA, Torre M, et al. Prevalence of Depression, Depressive Symptoms, and Suicidal Ideation Among Medical Students: A Systematic Review and Meta-Analysis. JAMA. 2016; 316(21):2214–2236. doi:10.1001/jama.2016.17324

Other Career Options

1. Association of Schools & Programs of Public Health.
   https://www.aspph.org/discover/

2. ExploreHealthCareers.org About this Site.
   https://explorehealthcareers.org/why-a-career-in-health/about-this-site/

For Parents

1. Association of American Medical Colleges Matriculating Student
   Questionnaire 2018 All Schools Summary Report.
   https://www.aamc.org/download/494044/data/msq2018report.pdf

Made in the USA
Lexington, KY
02 December 2019

57954312R00136